We long for disciples of Jesus
zeal and love. In this very h
Noakes takes us into 9 section
application and discussion m;
Christian life. Are you looking for something to put into the
hands of individuals and especially groups? Here it is. This is
a fresh gift for the church today and the disciples of tomorrow.

Simon Manchester
Senior Minister, St Thomas' Anglican Church, North
Sydney, 1989-2019

Christian Essentials is both expected and unlike anything else
available. The book covers what any good evangelical book
on discipleship would cover, and does so from an evangelical perspective. But it does this in a unique way. It does not
download information. It does not raise questions as riddles
for the reader to solve. Rather, the author walks beside the
reader in growing as a follower of Jesus. Each chapter begins
by making us curious and showing us, through the narratives
of Acts, why a particular aspect of discipleship matters. Then
follows a Bible study that does not give answers but guides
the reader through the text. Finally, Ken finishes each chapter with wise theological reflections to help sharpen and inte-
grate the disciple's thinking—and all this by relating wise and
sound thinking to the world we now inhabit.

This is a great resource to help grow disciples, not as mere
holders of knowledge but as ones who engage with their
world, capable of joyfully embracing the privilege of growing
as disciples of Christ.

Archie Poulos
Head, Department of Ministry
Director, Centre for Ministry Development
Moore Theological College, Sydney

Born out of Ken's pastoral heart and his desire for people to live in ways that honour Jesus, this book explores 9 aspects of Christian discipleship that Ken considers to be essential. Each chapter contains an in-depth Bible study followed by encouragement and instruction for those who seek to live faithfully for Christ. It's a Scripture-soaked treatment that challenges the reader to compare the life that Jesus calls us to with what the world offers, and shows how following and serving Jesus is so much better.

Wendy Lin
Book reviewer and blogger, Trinity Church Adelaide

I had the great privilege of serving alongside Ken Noakes at Holy Trinity Adelaide for many years. The image that sticks in my mind from that period is of Ken sitting in a coffee shop with two others looking at the Bible together—one a young or not-yet Christian and the other someone he was teaching to disciple others. The faces changed but the pattern didn't. The material in this creative book is not theoretical. It is the distilled experience of someone who has been consistently discipling others for decades. This is a resource that can be used to grow disciples. It combines thoughtful biblical insights with a wealth of accumulated pastoral experience. Ken demonstrates an excellent understanding of the pressures that new and not-so-new believers face. He answers real questions with what the Bible has to say, combined with wise understanding of human nature. This is a great addition for a pastor's toolbox.

Paul Harrington
Senior Network Pastor, The Trinity Network of Churches, Adelaide

This book is far more than just "a toolbox for living the Christian life" as the author humbly claims. Having read it, I would without any hesitation describe it as a handbook or manual that every Christian should use and follow. This book covers the foundational building blocks of a disciple's life, from the moment of a first personal encounter with Jesus through to the Christian maturity that the apostle Paul speaks of in Ephesians 4:13 and Colossians 1:28. It is certainly not a book that will be read once and shelved. It is designed to be used continuously by individuals and groups for self-evaluation, spiritual growth, and purposeful service in the kingdom. This book is a powerful tool for equipping Christians, who are called to be influencers in the world rather than being influenced by the world. This book is a timely gift to every Christ-follower and to the global church.

Dr Sam Stephens
President, India Gospel League

This book has the wonderful aim of helping us to be more godly Christians. The author is an experienced and admired pastor. He has thought deeply about how to communicate biblical teaching in an effective and readable way, and his work will be a blessing to those who study it.

Dr Peter Jensen
Anglican Archbishop of Sydney, 2001-2013

What does it look like to be a follower of Jesus in our complex world?

Written in an accessible and conversational style, Ken Noakes's book brings a refreshing approach to our understanding of discipleship in a complicated and post-faith culture, underpinned by relevant Scripture and everyday examples.

This book offers a 'toolbox' for understanding, considering and putting true discipleship into action, both for mature Christians and those who are still unsure.

Philip Bell OAM
Chairman, The Anglican Schools Corporation

This book is an invitation for all of us—enquirer, new believer, and those who've been Christian for a while—to equip ourselves with the tools for being effective disciples of Jesus. More detailed and comprehensive than an introductory course or short 'next steps', the creative chapter arrangement allows for deep examination of the fundamentals of the Christian faith. By the end of the book, participants will indeed have a full and useful toolbox.

Kara Hartley
Archdeacon for Women's Ministry, Anglican Church,
Diocese of Sydney

Ken is a gifted Bible teacher with extensive ministry experience in diverse contexts, both in Australia and in cross-cultural settings overseas. His ability to explain profound truths with clarity, confident in the authority of Scripture, has been evident in these different ministry contexts and similarly shines through in each chapter of *Christian Essentials*. I have no doubt this book will be of tremendous benefit to those new to the Christian faith, as well as to mature believers seeking to grow in their understanding of key biblical foundations that shape the life of disciples of Jesus.

John Lovell
Executive Director, Church Missionary Society, NSW and ACT

Christians must always be clear about the essentials of the Christian faith, and must hold on to them. Building on years of experience in pastoral ministry, Ken Noakes combines clarity, creativity and biblical faithfulness in defining and describing these essentials. The book is ideal for both the new believer and the older Christian who wants more certainty about what they believe and how they should live.

Mike Raiter
Director, Centre for Biblical Preaching, Melbourne

This is a splendid book on basic Christian discipleship. For the person wondering, "What will it look like for me to get started as a Christian and to begin to grow in my faith?", this book provides excellent answers. The Bible passages, short studies and imaginative reflection questions at the end of each chapter give valuable exercises to work on. The instructive material is thoroughly helpful. It is a useful resource for individuals and small groups.

William Taylor
Rector, St Helen's Bishopsgate, London

CHRISTIAN ESSENTIALS

*9 key characteristics
of every follower of Jesus*

KEN D NOAKES

SYDNEY · YOUNGSTOWN

Matthias Media
(St Matthias Press Ltd ACN 067 558 365)
Email: info@matthiasmedia.com.au
Internet: www.matthiasmedia.com.au
Please visit our website for current postal and telephone contact information.

Matthias Media (USA)
Email: sales@matthiasmedia.com
Internet: www.matthiasmedia.com
Please visit our website for current postal and telephone contact information.

ISBN 978 1 925424 83 6

Cover design and typesetting by Lankshear Design.

For Glad Ellen and Jan Michele:
you have been like Lois and Eunice to me

and

Naomi Anne,
my beloved

CONTENTS

INTRODUCTION

The word had got around. The crowds were gathering fast, and they were coming from everywhere.

Under some pressure to deal with their leader's growing fame, Jesus' disciples scrambled up a mountainside and gathered around him, setting the scene for possibly the most famous speech in history: the 'Sermon on the Mount' (Matthew 5-7).

With the vast crowds eagerly listening in, Jesus told his disciples what it means to follow him: "Let your light shine before others, that they may see your good deeds and glorify your Father in Heaven" (Matt 5:16).

What does a disciple of Jesus look like? A light. This statement from Jesus, "Let your light shine", is in many ways a perfect summary verse for this book. Christians live in a fallen and dark world, yet we are not to be like the fallen or dark world. We are to be a light.

Grasp this truth for a moment. So much about our secular world stresses the need to fit in. To conform. To be tolerant. There is, however, a key difference between being *in* the world and being *like* the world, and it is a difference that every Christian must understand and carefully live out.

But *how* do we do that? How do we fulfil our God-given task of being a light in a dark world?

You can think of this book as a bit like a toolbox for living the Christian life. When it comes to working with my hands, I have to admit I am not particularly gifted. My father-in-law's shed is largely a mystery to me. I walk in and see rows and rows of tools, supplies and equipment, stacked from floor to ceiling. If you were to ask me what most of the tools are for, it is likely that I would not have the foggiest idea!

Yet whenever I have a job to do, I know that in this shed are all the tools (and more) that I need to do it. The job may not be complicated, but it is important, and without the right tools it would be impossible to attempt or complete. So I grab a bit of this and a bit of that, and before I know it I have a car full of stuff. In my mind I have everything that I need to efficiently do the job.

But nothing could be further from the truth. In reality, I will fluff around, making an absolute mess, wasting all sorts of time and achieving very little. Why? Because I get so overwhelmed by everything before me that I do nothing right or well. I use the wrong tools in the wrong way, and then start to wonder why I even attempted the job at hand. Not efficient, and certainly not effective in any way.

Just like that moment when I walk into my father-in-law's tool shed, living the Christian life can sometimes feel overwhelming. But it doesn't have to be. This book puts before you nine elements—or 'tools'—that are essential for any person of faith in Jesus. It is an attempt to sort through the many and varied possibilities that are often associated with what it means to be a disciple of Jesus. Very often, the Christian person can become so burdened and distracted by the many good and valuable things that they could choose to do that they lose sight of some of those essential elements of following Jesus.

In each of the next nine chapters we will look at one aspect of Christian discipleship that should be a 'Christian essential' for any disciple of Jesus. Each concept presents us with a distinction between what the world expects of a person and what the Lord expects of his disciples.

1. Saved by grace
The world says: You earn your importance by what you do.
But God says: You are saved in Jesus, by grace, not by what you do.

2. Grounded in the Word
The world says: Listen to us. We'll offer you many different voices and opinions, and tell you what to believe.
But God says: Listen to me. I give you my word, the Bible, to show you how to live and why it is good to trust in me.

3. Faithful in prayer
The world says: Humanity knows best, and we can achieve whatever we set our minds to.
But God says: You need me, so talk to me in prayer. I will listen to you, and I will give you what is best.

4. Bold in witness
The world says: Watch yourself! Don't say anything we deem intolerant or confronting, or you'll be 'cancelled'.
But God says: Make Jesus famous, so that others will know how important it is that Jesus died for them.

5. Resilient in suffering

The world says: Don't worry, be happy; that should be your goal in life.

But God says: Persevere in the face of suffering and keep trusting me; your goals are not limited to this life.

6. Committed in membership

The world says: Put yourself first, and put others next—if it's convenient.

But God says: Love me above all else, and love others before yourself.

7. Loving in relationships

The world says: All you need is love—and we can define 'love' to be whatever we choose.

But God says: Love others in a way that is both pleasing and acceptable to me.

8. Godly in giving

The world says: The more you get, the happier you will be.

But God says: Give generously! Freely give, for you have been given much.

9. Fruitful in service

The world says: Take what you can get and look after yourself.

But God says: In love, find ways to do good works for others (even if it costs you).

• • •

This book is written for the person who wants to be essentially Christian. In each of our nine areas, the disciple is called to live out the gospel of Jesus Christ in a tangible way. And in doing so, the Christian is being a light in a dark place. Is that easy? Not always. But is it necessary? Absolutely! It is part of what it means to be an essential Christian.

If you are checking out the Christian faith, I hope these essentials will give you a window into what being a follower of Jesus looks like.

If you are new to the Christian faith, I hope these essentials will help to put in place the foundations so that you can intentionally set out well in your Christian walk.

If you have been following Jesus for some time, I hope these essentials will offer an opportunity to take stock of your Christian walk, and that they might even prompt some reassessment (if needed) to make sure you keep growing as a Christian.

And if you are doubting what it means to be a Christian—if you're wondering whether it's worth the effort—then I hope these essentials will be helpful prompts to reconsider what it means to live as a disciple of Jesus and why each element is important in the life of a believer.

Each chapter has three parts:

- **A voice from Acts**

  It was Jesus who taught his first disciples what was truly essential to live the Christian life. In the Acts of the Apostles, we see those disciples putting the essentials into practice. So each chapter of this book introduces its topic with a first-person retelling in the (imagined) voice of one of those first-century disciples.

- **A Bible study**
  This will take you straight to the source on each topic. The Bible study is designed to get you into the text of God's word so that you will be thinking through what God says about the topic. The study can easily be done on your own, one-to-one with someone else, or in a small group.

- **An exploration of the 'essential' topic**
  This final part of each chapter aims to address the topic in a clear and systematic way, showing you what each of the essentials should look like in the life of a believer and offering tips and suggestions for how you might put each one into practice.

· · ·

Come with me as we step into the shed and pull out only the tools that we must use, because Christians have a job to do—to shine the light of Jesus into a dark world—and we must do it effectively. I hope and pray that you will enjoy diving into the Bible and, under God, allowing it to shape you as an essential Christian.

1. SAVED BY GRACE

The world says:
You earn your importance by what you do.

But God says:
You are saved in Jesus, by grace, not by what you do.

A voice from Acts: "What must I do to be saved?"

Inspired by Acts 16:16-40

It had already been a strange day, and it only got stranger ...

I'm used to prisoners being abrupt or violent—that's all in a day's work. I am a jailer, after all. Lock them up, keep watch, feed them if necessary, get to the end of your shift—that's what keeps the bosses happy. Not much to it, really. Provided the prisoners are kept behind bars, the Roman authorities are happy with me. I help them maintain order by keeping the criminals off the street.

That is, if they're kept behind bars.

On this day, two new prisoners had been dragged in. 'Christians', they were called—I'd heard about them, how they were notorious for causing disruptions in the synagogues and marketplaces. The magistrate had ordered these two men, Paul and Silas, to be incarcerated—and it must have been for a serious crime, because we were told to put them in the inner high-security cell. We were told to shackle their feet, too, so there was no way they could do a runner.

These two prisoners were strange. Everyone could see it; even the other prisoners. We could hear their voices floating out from the cell, but not the usual cries of fury or anguish. They were singing. Hymns! (Who *does* that?) And then they seemed quite content to do a lot of praying. I remember thinking, "I don't know who they think is going to help them now!" But when we looked in on them, sitting there shackled to the wall, they were ... different. Calm. Peaceful. *Joyful*. "Each to their own", I said, and shrugged.

And then it happened. Around midnight, the walls began to shake. There was a deafening sound as the earthquake buckled the floors and sent cracks shooting through the walls. The wind blew out the torches ... and the cell doors were dislodged from their hinges. All of them.

This was bad news. I have one key performance indicator—keep the prisoners locked up! And if I can't do that one job, then I pay for it with my life. Harsh, I know—but that's the deal.

And now an earthquake had opened the cells.

The next bit is a bit hazy. So much happened, so quickly.

When I realized that the prison was open, I knew I had a horrible choice to make. To the Romans, saying "An earthquake set the prisoners free" would sound pretty lame.

I tried to slow my breathing. What to do? Run away? Was that the answer? But what about my wife, my kids? I had to focus. Think. Act.

I grabbed my sword. My arms shook. I raised the sword to my chest. "I'll have to fall on my sword—better that than face the Romans or put my family at risk", I thought. "I've got no choice. Why did this have to happen to me?"

Then came that voice—a voice I'll never forget—out of the rubble, through the thick dust, calling urgently in the darkness: "Don't harm yourself! We are all here!"

I called for lights. "Of course!" I thought. I was so relieved. I had forgotten about the shackles! I had them locked by the feet. They couldn't leave! But as I rushed into their cell and shakily held the torch up in front of them I saw the strangest thing of all. Not only had the earthquake knocked the doors from their hinges, it had somehow loosened everybody's chains. How could an earthquake do that?

The prisoners were all free; but they were still there!

Why?

I looked at Paul and Silas with my mouth open. If I was a prisoner and my shackles suddenly dropped off and the cell doors swung open, I would take it as an invitation to hot-foot it out of there—but not these men. My body started shaking even more violently. If indeed all the prisoners were still there, my life was saved. I fell to my knees in front of them.

I thought about those men—their notoriety, their hymns, their prayers. And it was at that point it dawned on me: I needed something more than just having my physical life saved. I needed the salvation they had! It was personal. It was powerful. It was beyond anything that I could do for myself. I got to my feet and brought them out of the cell.

"Sirs, what must I do to be saved?" I blurted out.

And I will never, ever forget the answer!

"Believe in the Lord Jesus, and you will be saved—you and your whole household."

Bible study

Reflection/discussion points

- How does our world measure success? Consider the different secular, day-to-day spheres of your life (e.g. schooling, parenting, work): in what ways is a person seen to be valuable within these spheres?

- What do you think it looks like to be 'a success' as a Christian?

Pray that this study would help you to hear the word of God and respond to it in a way that is pleasing to him.

Read Ephesians 2:1-10

Suggestion: Be creative—find some paper and draw a picture that depicts this passage.

1. Who is this passage written to? Who does this passage critique?

2. What are the characteristics of one who is disobedient? What are the consequences of disobedience?

3. Opposite to being dead in transgressions and sins, God has "made us alive with Christ" (v 5). Why? By what means did God do this?

4. Describe 'grace' as explained in this passage.

5. Why has God "seated us with [Jesus] in the heavenly realms" (v 6)?

6. This passage indicates that it is by grace *through faith* that one is saved (v 8). Where does the passage say faith comes from?

7. What kind of 'work' does God ask of us?

Implications

- How should this passage shape a person saved by grace in Christ?

- Is it possible to earn our salvation by doing good things? What does this passage suggest about this idea?

- Now that you've read this passage, revisit the reflection point at the beginning of the Bible study: What do you think it looks like to be 'a success' as a Christian?

Suggestions for prayer

- Give thanks to God for his gift—salvation through faith in Christ Jesus.
- Ask God to help you value what he has done over what the world says you should do.

God's gracious work

According to Acts 16, the Philippian jailer and his whole family listened to the word of the Lord as spoken by the apostle Paul, accepted it, and were baptized as a sign that they had been saved (Acts 16:32-40).

Christians are people who believe in the Lord Jesus. They are saved not by what *they* have done but by what *he* has done. Jesus' greatest gift is his salvation—which is why Christians can clearly and confidently say that they are 'saved by grace'.

This is a fundamental starting point.

Let me explain.

Being a 'person of faith in Jesus' is not a status that is earned or established by some wonderful deed. Christians are not saved by the good things that they do, or by the sufferings that they endure, or by the things that they go without, as if heavenly credit points are accumulated in some way.

Salvation by grace is a truth that is one of the most liked but most badly applied truths of the Bible—and a truth that people often find difficult to accept.

It is **liked** because it speaks of God's gracious work to save.

If you took a person who was, at best, an enemy and gave them everything as if they were your best friend, then you would have to say that was gracious—an unwarranted, and therefore extraordinarily gracious, gift. That is what God has done in saving a Christian.

It is **badly applied** because of the way many take this grace for granted.

It is making a faulty assumption to assert that because God is loving he will save everyone. And further, it is a fallacy to think that because God has saved, people no longer need to obey God.

It can also be **hard to accept** God's gift of grace. But why is this the case?

The concept of our need to accept God's gift of grace is one of the many points where the Bible is totally out of step with our society!

Romans 5 helps us:

¹ Therefore, since we have been justified through faith, we have peace with God through our Lord Jesus Christ, ² through whom we have gained access by faith into this grace in which we now stand. And we boast in the hope of the glory of God. ³ Not only so, but we also glory in our sufferings, because we

know that suffering produces perseverance; ⁴ perseverance, character; and character, hope. ⁵ And hope does not put us to shame, because God's love has been poured out into our hearts through the Holy Spirit, who has been given to us.

⁶ You see, at just the right time, when we were still powerless, Christ died for the ungodly. ⁷ Very rarely will anyone die for a righteous person, though for a good person someone might possibly dare to die. ⁸ But God demonstrates his own love for us in this: While we were still sinners, Christ died for us.

⁹ Since we have now been justified by his blood, how much more shall we be saved from God's wrath through him! ¹⁰ For if, while we were God's enemies, we were reconciled to him through the death of his Son, how much more, having been reconciled, shall we be saved through his life! ¹¹ Not only is this so, but we also boast in God through our Lord Jesus Christ, through whom we have now received reconciliation. (Rom 5:1-11)

A confronting truth

The first reason that *salvation by grace* is out of step with the world is because the Bible says that we can do nothing to earn favour with God. We are saved by faith, *not our works.*

Being "justified through faith" (v 1) is a fancy way of saying that a person's relationship with God has been put right. How does that happen? The answer is there for all to read: "through faith … through our Lord Jesus Christ".

The "therefore" at the beginning of the verse tells us that the writer is making the argument based on something already written in the letter. The apostle Paul wrote this letter to the Christians in Rome, many of whom would have had Jewish origins, meaning they were descendants of Israel and would have grown up knowing the history in the

Old Testament of how God had saved them.

A quick history lesson: the Father of Israel, a guy named Abraham, is the one who heard the original promises from God that he would save his people—in fact, that is the topic of Romans 4 (the chapter immediately before the passage above). Paul explains how God had credited Abraham as righteous: "What does Scripture say? 'Abraham believed God, and it was credited to him as righteousness'" (Rom 4:3; cf. Gen 15:6). What is significant here is that at the time Abraham was credited as righteous, he had not *done* anything that would give him credit. He had no law to follow (that came later with Moses). He had no birthmark; no distinct sign that marked him as special (circumcision—which was done to mark out a person of Israel—came later). And yet, Abraham was declared righteous.

The point: God declared Abraham to be right with him on the basis of faith, not on the basis of any effort on Abraham's part.

God justified the Christians in Rome, and justifies Christians today, through their faith in Jesus, not because of any human effort.

That is a very different picture from the way our society thinks and operates. Imagine what it would be like to receive something good without having to earn it. To be graded with top marks at school without having to do any homework or sit any exams. To be awarded top marks at university without submitting an essay or handing in an assignment. To be promoted and remunerated at work without having to sit through a performance review or meet any KPIs!

God's gift of salvation is not gained by our efforts; it is received through faith in Christ.

It is about hope

The second reason that *salvation by grace* is totally out of step with the world has to do with hope.

There is a connection drawn between grace and hope in verse 2 of the Romans passage above, which says that "we have gained access by faith into this grace in which we now stand. And we *boast in the hope* of the glory of God." (Some translations use the word 'rejoice' instead of 'boast'. Either way, what it means is that the Christian can really celebrate this hope.)

Christians have access *by faith into this grace in which we now stand*. Can you see that this is a present reality for those in faith? They "now stand".

Our world tends to think of hope as sort of like wishful thinking, like winning the lotto ("I hope I win the jackpot"), but that is not the Bible's view of hope at all. *Hope* is a sure thing because of God's grace in Jesus.

Consider for a moment what that means for the person of faith—they can rejoice in the *certain* "hope of the glory of God". Every time a person gets baptized (like the Philippian jailer in Acts 16), and every time a person declares that they are a follower of Jesus, they are declaring that they accept what Jesus has done for them and also what that means for their glorious future. They rejoice in hope.

Does that mean that a Christian should expect everything in life to be roses? Not at all! Christian hope is not simply present when things are good; hope also has relevance when things are not so good. Read on in our passage. Verses 3-4 say that "we also *glory in our sufferings*, because we know that suffering produces perseverance; perseverance, character; and character, hope".

Is that not strange to our ears? Glory in suffering! (In fact, the Greek word for 'glory' here is actually the same word as 'boast' in the previous verse! If we can boast or rejoice in hope, we can also boast or rejoice in suffering.) Who wants to rejoice in their sufferings?

It is strange, because the hope on offer in our world is lost when suffering comes. If all we live for is what can be offered in the here and now, then at some point that will be found to be wanting. Suffering, for any reason at all, is one such point.

With Jesus, suffering cannot take away Christian hope, because even if suffering leads drastically to the point of death, there is more. There is peace forever with God.

It is not uncommon to hear reports of Christians suffering for their faith. There are many countries around the world in which those most targeted are those who hold to a Christian faith. To be attacked, to be beaten, to be exiled or even to be killed is hardly something to rejoice in. Yet this experience does not mean hope is void—in fact, those who do suffer will often say that it is at those times when hope is most important. Chapter 5, 'Resilient in suffering', will consider this topic in more detail.

If Christian hope is simply 'wishful thinking' then Christians should be pitied more than anyone. Conversely, if worldly hope is to be taken seriously, then it must find an answer for suffering.

What we don't like to admit

The third reason that salvation by grace is out of step with the world is because it tells us something about ourselves that, deep down, we know is true but do not like to admit.

Verse 6 in the Romans passage identifies me as someone who is "ungodly". Verse 8 calls me a "sinner". It's not a very popular notion!

I quite like thinking of myself as a good person, and I am sure that, given the opportunity, you also would like to be seen as a good person. Generally, we are good, give or take the occasional traffic infringement or swearword! Yes, we are good people! But I am not sure anyone would want to put their hand up and say they were perfect. And that is the point.

So if we are not perfect, then we are sinners. This passage is reminding us that deep down we are ungodly and sinners.

Paint me with the brush of sin and you paint a portrait of an unrighteous man. I wish I could say otherwise, but I am a sin masterpiece!

So how do 'good' people, if not by their own efforts, come to have peace with the one who is perfect? How do the unrighteous become righteous? The answer is that Jesus took our place: "While we were still sinners, Christ died for us" (v 8).

Jesus did not need to die *for* a righteous man; he had to die *as* a righteous man—in order that we 'good' people might be made completely righteous in God's sight.

This is the greatest trade in history. On the cross, Jesus (the perfectly righteous Son of God) took my place (the place of a tainted and unrighteous sinner), and died so that I would be set free. It was his effort, not mine. His life, for mine. Jesus paid what he didn't owe, for what I owed and couldn't pay.

Why was that so necessary?

Simply, as verses 9-11 above show us, this is everyone. Without Jesus we are God's enemies. Being an enemy of anyone is hardly a pleasant notion. Being an enemy of the God of the universe should be terrifying! And without someone to step between us and God, we are in the firing line of his wrath. There is absolutely nothing comforting about that picture.

It is into that reality that God's grace comes: "For if, while we were God's enemies, we were reconciled to him through the death of his Son, how much more, having been reconciled, shall we be saved through his life!" (v 10).

Faith, works and grace

What does it mean to be saved through faith by God's grace?

It means that God, through Jesus, and only through Jesus, has made the effort to save us. It is his gift and it is freely given. That's grace.

When someone works at a job, they receive payment for what they have done. They have earned their pay. We would never call that pay cheque a gift. By works, we get what we deserve. That is exactly why 'faith' is the opposite to 'works'— by *works* we get what we deserve, but in *faith* we get what we *don't* deserve.

A Christian is saved through faith by grace.

Faith, obedience and grace

While *faith* can be contrasted with *works*, there is another dimension to consider. *Faith* can also be contrasted with *disobedience*. And that is why when someone becomes a person of faith, the right response is to obey Jesus. After all, why would you trust Jesus to remove your sin and guilt before God if you were only going to hold on to sin and continue to disobey God day after day?

When Jesus started his public ministry as recorded in Mark 1, his first words were these: "The time has come … The kingdom of God has come near. Repent and believe the good news!" (v 15).

Jesus calls people to repent (turn to him) and to believe (place their trust in him). *Repentance* involves seeing sin for the deceitful and deadly thing that it really is, and turning *away* from it. *Belief* in Jesus involves seeing Jesus for the gracious and powerful Saviour that he really is, and turning *to* him.

Faith places these two acts together in a person's salvation—repentance and belief are two sides of the same 'faith coin', if you like.

Have you ever noticed that when you turn from something you turn in two ways?

Suppose you are walking towards the front door of your house when you suddenly remember that you have left your bag on the bench. When you turn to go back to the bench you also turn away from the front door. Every turning involves a turning *from* something *to* something.

That is what a saving faith looks like. It involves *turning from* the horror of sin (without which you will stay out of step and not at peace with God, who will hold you to account) and it involves *turning to* trust and hope in Jesus (who brings you in step with God and to peace with him).

Now let me try to explain why repenting and believing in Christ is not a 'work'.

Repenting and believing in Jesus, if done solely as a

human action, would do nothing *if* Jesus had not already paid the price. But when you repent and believe in Jesus, it is as if you are coming to him with an empty hand and saying, "I offer myself not by merit, as if I have anything to offer, but in humility, relying totally on what you have done". By faith, we recognize that it is because of Jesus that salvation forever is even on offer, and it is by God's grace and only by his grace that we are saved.

What does a Christian look like?

So for someone who is indeed *saved by grace*, what should that change about the way you live your life?

A Christian is someone who has moved from being out of step with God to now being someone who is in step with God through Jesus. Or to put that another way, a Christian is someone who has moved from being in step with the world to now being someone who is out of step with the world. So:

- Don't think that being good, or working hard for God, can give you more credit. The best line of credit has already been offered in Jesus alone.
- Don't take the gift of salvation for granted. Instead, live a life that is worthy of the gift that has so generously been given. And that will look like a sinner who rejoices in the hope of the glory of God and rejoices in whatever suffering they might experience for being in Jesus Christ.
- Be more concerned about the security you have in Christ than you are concerned about the security you have in the world. There will always be a temptation to rest in what the world offers, but it will only be a temporary rest.

- Be obedient to Jesus. There will be a temptation to use the excuse "Because I am saved by grace, I don't have to do anything that Christ asks of me" (of course, we wouldn't say it like that—we would be much more nuanced or subtle). You may be tempted to think to yourself, "I don't have to be involved in service, because I know I have already been saved by grace", but this is a self-deception and a misunderstanding of grace. As Christians we should be concerned about being saved people who take obedience to our Saviour very seriously. There will be more about being fruitful in service in chapter 9.

What's best next?

- What aspects of your thinking and your behaviour should be changed as a result of reflecting on this 'essential' Christian quality?

- What step can you take this week to make that change?

Pray about it.

2. GROUNDED IN THE WORD

The world says: Listen to us. We'll offer you many different voices and opinions, and tell you what to believe.

But God says: Listen to me. I give you my word, the Bible, to show you how to live and why it is good to trust in me.

A voice from Acts: "It all started because I read his book."

Inspired by Acts 8:26-40

I had never read anything like this before!

The words were rich, resonant, tragic; they sang of a most unfortunate person—a man slaughtered like a sheep, who didn't raise a word in his own defence; a man silent like a lamb being shorn for the first time. He was humiliated. He was deprived of justice. He was childless. I didn't know this man; and not many I knew, even among my own people, had suffered like this. And yet, somehow, the tragic words sang to me. I read them aloud to savour their sound.

My long journeys by chariot are often good times to read and think. I am honoured to work for the Ethiopian Queen, making sure my people are provided for well. So much is asked of me as head official overseeing the royal treasury. Yet I know that not all eunuchs are given such respect and privilege—like the freedom I had just been granted to travel to Jerusalem to worship. I know I am in a fortunate position.

I was on my way home from Jerusalem, and I'd pulled over to rest and to read. I can't even remember how I came to be in possession of the scroll I was reading, but I have to say, it blew my mind. It was the whole book of Isaiah, a section of the Jewish Scriptures. I had heard of it, but it was pretty unusual for an Ethiopian eunuch to have access to such a book. And as I read it, I was thinking, "But why does this captivate me so much? Who is this suffering man?" It didn't make sense.

"Do you understand what you are reading?"

I jumped and looked around. The voice had come from a man standing beside my chariot. He was a little breath-less, as though he had been running; as though he had an urgent message to deliver. He must have heard me reading the words from Isaiah aloud as he approached.

I looked back at the scroll. "How can I understand", I said, "unless someone explains it to me? Please, come up and sit with me."

So this man, Philip, jumped into the chariot and began to speak as we travelled slowly along the road.

I told him about the suffering man I had been reading about. "Tell me, please, who is the prophet talking about, himself or someone else?"

Philip began to speak. My word! Isaiah was talking about a man called Jesus. No wonder I was captivated. Here were words written generations earlier, all about a man who lived in my own generation, who died for those who he came to save! Who died for *me*—a eunuch, a non-Jew, a foreigner!

And it all came together for me then. My journey, the scroll I was reading, Philip's appearance at just the right time, the wonderful news about Jesus ... I had to give my life to Jesus right away! Seeing some water beside the road, I said to Philip, "Look, here is water. What can stand in the way of my being baptized?"

We stopped, and right then and there I stepped into the puddle, and Philip baptized me in the name of Jesus. I turned to thank Philip—but he was gone!

I got back into the chariot, bewildered but overjoyed, and continued my journey, rejoicing that I had met Philip and found Jesus, my new Lord and Saviour.

Before my journey I was a proud official serving a powerful queen; but now I serve and worship the king of all—and it all started because I read his book.

Bible study

Reflection/discussion points

- There are many voices calling for our attention. How does society determine who or what to listen to?

- "Everyone is entitled to their own opinion." How does this mantra both help and hinder a Christian who wants to hold firmly to what the Bible says?

Pray that this study would help you to hear the word of God and respond to it in a way that is pleasing to him.

Read 2 Timothy 3:10-4:8

Suggestion: Read through this passage several times using different Bible versions. Note any obvious differences.

1. This passage is written by the apostle Paul to instruct his younger brother in faith, Timothy. What is he asking of Timothy? Why is this so important?

2. What good comes from knowing holy Scripture? Why?

3. Why "continue in" the Scriptures (3:14)? What is the end purpose?

4. Western society values the importance of teaching and training, but is not so favourable towards rebuking or correcting (see 3:16). What would be lost if Bible believers focused only on teaching and training and avoided rebuking and correcting?

   Note: These qualities have both doctrinal and ethical implications. "Teaching" and "rebuking" may relate to helping the Christian think rightly (doctrine), whereas "correcting" and "training" may help the Christian to act rightly (ethics).

5. Paul calls Timothy to "preach the word" (4:2). Does this apply only to Timothy as a leader or to all believers? What does this command imply for the listener?

6. Given that the context here is to "preach the word" to believers (those in the Christian faith), why does Paul tell Timothy to "be prepared in season and out of season …" (4:2)?

7. What is the threat that Timothy will encounter?

Implications

- What warnings or cautions does this passage highlight for believers? How should a believer safeguard themselves from becoming someone who has "itching ears" (4:3)?

- What would be at stake if our society prevented God's voice from being heard (for example, legislated against the public reading or teaching of the Bible)?

- What would be lost if the Christian chose to listen first to the voices of the world before listening to God's voice?

- What practices or routines could be put in place to encourage and promote your spiritual discipline of Bible reading?

Suggestions for prayer

Tip: Take God's word so seriously that you ensure that it shapes your week. For example, read a little bit each day; give priority to occasions when God's word is taught and discussed (e.g. church, Bible study group, one-to-one with someone); pre-read the passage that will be preached on each week so that you have it in mind when you meet with God's people. There is more on this in the following chapter.

Shaped by the Word

Christians are people of the word—the written and spoken word. I am not just saying that Christians are bookworms; I'm saying that at ground zero, a Christian is shaped by God's word. It informs, it motivates, it comforts, it rebukes, it sharpens, it directs—and it does so all by the power of the Holy Spirit.

If you have recently become a Christian and you open up a Bible, you will find yourself faced with a big volume of 2 testaments, 66 books, 1,189 chapters, 31,103 verses, and you may think, "Is it worth it? How do I read it? Where do I start?"[1]

---

1   You may be interested to know that the original manuscripts of the Bible did not contain chapter numbers, verse numbers or subheadings at all. The Old Testament manuscripts, written largely in Hebrew, were divided into paragraphs (each called a 'parashah') to break the text up for its reading in the synagogue across the year. Chapter and verse numbers were introduced later—between the 12th and 14th centuries. For the New Testament manuscripts, differing number conventions were used; it was not until the publication of the Geneva Bible in 1560 that a universal convention for both chapters and verses was accepted. It is that convention that we see in most modern-day versions of the Bible. As for the subheadings, they have been added by the translation committees for each version of the Bible—hence the fact that they differ between Bible versions.

And if you have been a Christian for a while, then you may recognize the struggle it often is to read the Bible regularly and well—to let the Bible work on your heart and challenge your mind and change your behaviour. In short, to shape your life.

These are good concerns.

Without the Bible, a person will struggle to grasp the fundamental Christian truth that while they were still a sinner, Christ died for them (Rom 5:8). Without the Bible, it is impossible to understand what it really means to be Christian.

In this chapter, we'll look at how we know God—Father, Son and Spirit—and how we know what he wants of us. The simple answer is that the Bible tells us so.

God makes himself known

If 'God' is truly almighty, the Creator, the reason for existence, the first cause of all things—as would be the nature of anyone who would claim to be 'god'—then how do we know that? How does he make himself known?

There are three ways.

1. Look around

The world around us has to be a source of information about God if he is indeed the source of all life; so the first way we can know about God is by looking around and examining what we see.

Naturally, we can attribute the good things that we see to God. And interestingly, we should also attribute the bad things that we see to him.

The reality is that because good things *don't* cause pain

and suffering, then it is often those things that we overlook. Yet when it comes to the bad things, and the things that affect us and limit our experience or existence, then we pay much more attention.

Don't be surprised when people say that they don't want to follow a 'god' who would allow suffering—because it is abundantly clear that there is much suffering in the world.

Be that as it may, let us consider for a moment some of the wonderful things that we see in the world. There are many things that are completely beyond our ability to even fathom. Consider the expanse of the universe in which we live, with the billions of stars the size of our sun. Reflect for a moment on the beauty of our land with its mountains and valleys, forests, rivers and deserts, which all work together to sustain life (and at times take life). Bring to mind the vastness of the oceans and the lakes, and the depths of the seas which hide creatures that continue to amaze us (like the great blue whale) or terrify us (like the white pointer shark). Marvel at the wonder of wildlife with its kangaroos and its eagles and its elephants and its lions—not to mention the awkwardness of the giraffe or the emu or the hippopotamus, or the hideous elegance of the snake! And cherish the gift of people from newborn to old age, each different from one another and varied in appearance, colour, language, size, temperament, fingerprint and ability. There are wonderful things that are on display in this world and they come from somewhere—or, more appropriately, some*one*.

In fact, the Bible tells us as much:

The heavens declare the glory of God;
    the skies proclaim the work of his hands.

Day after day they pour forth speech;
   night after night they reveal knowledge. (Ps 19:1-2)

… what may be known about God is plain to them, because God has made it plain to them. For since the creation of the world God's invisible qualities—his eternal power and divine nature— have been clearly seen, being understood from what has been made, so that people are without excuse. (Rom 1:19-20)

The very qualities of God's own life are shown through the world and the universe that he has fashioned. God's greatness, order, power and beauty are shown in the created world. And so you can look at the world and learn something about God. Can I suggest that rather than taking the good with the bad, we might consider how to take the bad with the good— because God has given us an awful lot of good to see?

2. Look at ourselves

Another way we can learn something about God is to look at ourselves: how he made us!

If he can make an Ed Sheeran or a Meryl Streep or a Cristiano Ronaldo or a Serena Williams or even you—then there has to be something amazing about him.

How many things about our own bodies should amaze us? Think of our eyes and ears and hearts and brains—and how, somehow, they all work together without having to replace batteries every six months or so.

Just as with the rest of creation, they tell us something about God—about his wisdom and greatness and power.

Psalm 139 expresses it well:

For you created my inmost being;
   you knit me together in my mother's womb.

> I praise you because I am fearfully and wonderfully made;
>> your works are wonderful,
>> I know that full well.
> My frame was not hidden from you
>> when I was made in the secret place,
>> when I was woven together in the depths of the earth.
> Your eyes saw my unformed body;
>> all the days ordained for me were written in your book
>> before one of them came to be. (Ps 139:13-16)

And then, when we allow ourselves to be totally honest, there's that deep inner understanding that distinguishes between right and wrong—the voice that screams every time we do something that we shouldn't, or don't do something that we should. God's holiness, righteousness, goodness and justice are shown through the intimate and personal inner voice that we all have. Our consciences (although flawed) bear testimony to the fact that God is there and knows better than we do.

Now those two ways (the world around us and the people we are) tell us something generally about God. But they are not definitive. We learn something of the *quality* and *nature* of God, but they don't tell us *who* God is.

If we left our discussion about 'God' here, you could quite easily assert that all 'gods' are the same—because there is no way of telling the difference. We need a third way to know God.

3. Listen to what he says

And here is where the Bible comes into its own. The third way—the best way and the only true way—to know God is to listen to him!

One of the first things that we learn about God in the opening chapter of the Bible is that he talks. "In the beginning God created ..." (Gen 1:1).

And how did he do that?

By his word:

> And God *said*, "Let there be light" ... And God *said*, "Let there be a vault between the waters [the sky]" ... And God *said*, "Let the water under the sky be gathered to one place, and let dry ground appear ..." (Gen 1:3-9)

And so it goes on, for seven days (Gen 1:1-2:3).

Each of the special acts of creation comes about by *the word* of God. What he creates is new and wonderful and he does that by uttering his words.

If the significance of that is lost on you, give it a go! Test the power of your words. Create something by your words and only your words: "Let there be a ham sandwich!" How did you go? I think I can guess.

God speaks, and it is by his word that things happen—so it should not be a surprise that one of the most precious and important possessions we have in all of life is our Bible.

When the Bible speaks, God speaks.

When you listen to what the Bible is saying, you are listening to God talking to you.

When you do what the Bible asks you to do, you are being obedient to God.

In 2 Timothy 3:16-17 (which we looked at in the Bible study above) the apostle Paul tells Timothy, his younger brother in faith, something about the Bible that we should never forget:

All Scripture is God-breathed and it is useful for teaching, rebuking, correcting and training in righteousness, so the servant of God may be thoroughly equipped for every good work.

All Scripture—not just part of Scripture, but *all* of it—comes from God. We should see the Bible as a different kind of book to any other book there is. This book comes with the authority of God.

And that Scripture is *God-breathed*—which is a way of saying that it comes from God's own mouth. It is him speaking, and it is him speaking to us! He speaks and breathes out the very books that form the Scriptures that we have.

So, when we take these three ways that God makes himself known, and we consider *what he has done* (his actions that we see generally in his world) and add *what he has said* (his explanation that we can read specifically in his word), we will find that we have *his revelation* (his clearest possible self-portrait).

Vincent van Gogh (the Dutch post-impressionist painter working in the late 1800s) famously painted over 35 self-portraits, and just about everything we know about his appearance comes from these artworks—his red hair, green eyes, bushy beard and angular face. Given that van Gogh was unknown in his lifetime, art critics across the years have studied these works and drawn many and various opinions about van Gogh's personality. His facial expressions were often restrained, focused, serious. His clothes and hair were at times unkempt. Two of his portraits show him to have a bandaged left ear. There is value in looking at what van Gogh painted when trying to understand this remarkable artist.

Yet it is when we add to those works the more than 600

letters that van Gogh wrote to his younger brother that we gain a far greater understanding of who Vincent was, what he valued, who he loved, his art theories, his burdens, his cares and concerns, his injuries (his left ear was bandaged because he attempted to cut it off), his state of mind, his poverty, and more. Those letters are eloquent, expressive, and written in three different languages (Dutch, French and English). Putting his actions and his words together help us to better understand not only a remarkable artist, but a remarkable man.

God does indeed make himself known in the world by his actions, but we need his words to properly and more fully understand both his actions and God himself.

Can you see the problem of judging what God does in the world *without* considering what he says in his Scripture?

How can the Bible be from humans but also from God?

So how is it that the Bible arrived in the form in which we have it?

Paul is again helpful. With Timothy, he writes to the church in Thessalonica, saying:

> And we also thank God continually because, when you received the word of God, which you heard from us, you accepted it not as a human word, but as it actually is, the word of God, which is indeed at work in you who believe. (1 Thess 2:13)

The word of God that was "received" was handed down *by* God *through* those who had first heard it, and their job was to tell others. Of course, that begs the questions: How can the Bible be from men but really from God? How can we be sure that the humans who spoke and wrote actually had the spoken and written word that God wanted them to express?

2 Peter 1 is also helpful. Peter, speaking as one who received Scripture and recorded it, says this:

> For we did not follow cleverly devised stories when we told you about the coming of our Lord Jesus Christ in power, but we were eyewitnesses of his majesty. (2 Pet 1:16)

How was it that they were eyewitnesses of this? Read on:

> [Jesus] received honour and glory from God the Father when the voice came to him from the Majestic Glory, saying, "This is my Son, whom I love; with him I am well pleased." (2 Pet 1:17)

How amazing would that be? From the heavens, a voice comes and announces something to the world. And there is Peter watching on. If you were standing there and suddenly a voice like that spoke and it spoke about a person, you would look to see who it was. Extraordinary.

Twice during Jesus' time on earth he was identified by a voice from heaven booming out this confirmation. The first time was at his **baptism**. In Matthew 3, Jesus came with the crowds into the Jordan River to John the Baptist. As soon as he was baptized, the heavens opened and the Spirit of God descended in the form of a dove and rested on Jesus, and with that a voice from heaven rang out: "This is my Son, whom I love; with him I am well pleased" (Matt 3:17; cf. Mark 1:11; Luke 3:22).

The second time was at what is called the **transfiguration**—and it was this event that Peter was probably talking about in 2 Peter 1. It is recorded in Matthew, Mark and Luke.

Peter, James and John, disciples who all went on to record Scripture, went up with Jesus onto a mountain and in front of them Jesus was suddenly 'transfigured' and shone like the sun. With him appeared Moses and Elijah from the Old Testament, and then from the heavens a voice called out, "This is my Son, whom I love; with him I am well pleased. Listen to him!" (Matt 17:5; cf. Mark 9:7; Luke 9:35).

Peter (along with James and John) stood as one of the eyewitnesses to this amazing event. As Jesus' constant companions, Peter, James and John also witnessed the many words, actions and miracles of Jesus. And it is this Jesus that Peter is testifying about.

Peter says:

> We also have the prophetic message as something completely reliable, and you will do well to pay attention to it … Above all, you must understand that no prophecy of Scripture came about by the prophet's own interpretation of things. For prophecy never had its origin in the human will, but prophets, though human, spoke from God as they were carried along by the Holy Spirit. (2 Pet 1:19-21)

He is saying that the Holy Spirit of God, who lives in all believers, did a special work in taking the eyewitnesses' accounts and producing Scripture. It is God's way of using human writers to record his words for the benefit of those who pay attention to it.

It helps us to understand why the individual books of the Bible are so different and yet the Bible is so united in its overall message. Moses, David, Isaiah, Jeremiah, Matthew, John, Peter, Luke, Paul, James and others wrote—and God used their individual styles to communicate exactly what he wanted recorded so that the generations that would follow would have his words to read.

The fact that the Bible—encompassing both Old and New Testaments—has approximately 40 human writers, in three different languages, writing over a 2,000-year period of history, all telling God's story of redemption in a way that connects the dots from creation to salvation through to a new creation, is in itself a marker of God's hand.

In the Bible, we have the most historically attested ancient documents in all history (see appendix A for more information regarding the reliability of the Bible).

Because the Bible is *what it is* (God's own word), it can *do what it does* (teach, rebuke, correct and train its readers). And so we should not be surprised that because the Bible is what it is (God's own word), it is enabled to do what it does (grow us in the way God wants us to grow).

Essential for a Christian should be a willingness to listen to, and obey, God's voice in the Bible over that of the world.

What does a Christian do with the Bible?

What place should the Bible have in a Christian's life? An essential Christian discipline is to **read or listen to the Bible regularly through the week**. It would be a shame if the secular news cycle (or worse, social media) was able to speak more loudly into your life each week than the word of God.

The battle to put *the word of God* before *the word of the world* is ongoing. Each time you read or watch the news (an activity which in itself is not wrong), you subject yourself to the opinions of the journalists. It is not difficult for truth to get lost or skewed in the pursuit of a growing readership or audience, and journalism is often driven by a predetermined agenda or bias. Our secular media are rarely accountable to anything but their ratings.

So as Christians we need to **find—or make—time to read the word of God**. Get a Bible app, follow a reading plan, print out a book of the Bible, download an MP3 of the Bible, keep your Bible close. Then, as you travel to school or work, or when you are waiting for your computer to start up, or over breakfast or lunch or before bed—read and listen to it! For me, following a reading plan that means I work in order through passages from both the Old and New Testaments has always been helpful—it may be as little as a verse, or as much as a chapter at each go. I read. I think, "What is God saying here?" I pray. Perhaps you could ask some Christian friends or elders what they have done over the years. What works for you may be different to what works for the next person.

Also give some thought to where you **digest the word of God**. If there are places that will help you do that, pursue them more eagerly than you might a gym membership! Church, a Bible study group, reading with a friend, attending Bible teaching conferences or events—protect those times and give them priority so that your life will continue to be shaped and formed by God's word.

And **obey the word of God**. Reading it is great, but it means nothing if you don't do what it says. How do you allow it to shape you, to change your thinking, to challenge your worldview or that of others around you? There are many things that the Bible asks of us, all under the banner of grace. Those who hear it and obey it are those who are equipped to do every good work for the glory of God.

Happy reading.

What's best next?

- What aspects of your thinking and your behaviour should be changed as a result of reflecting on this 'essential' Christian quality?

- What step can you take this week to make that change?

Pray about it.

3. FAITHFUL IN PRAYER

The world says: Humanity knows best, and we can
achieve whatever we set our minds to.

But God says: You need me, so talk to me in prayer.
I will listen to you, and I will give you what is best.

A voice from Acts: "All we could do was lift our voices to God in prayer."

Inspired by Acts 4:1-31

The earth moved!

If ever I start thinking that prayer is weak, all I need to do is remember back to that day, to that prayer meeting, when the ground shook and, by the power of the Holy Spirit, we spoke the word of God boldly.

Here's how it all came about: the apostles had been healing and teaching and proclaiming that Jesus had risen from the dead, and our number had grown to about five thousand—can you believe that? Five thousand new believers in such a short time! I know—it seems so far-fetched! But then again, the news about Jesus coming back to life was even more incredible, but true. Now anything seemed possible. The resurrection had changed everything.

There was such joy in the city. So many who heard the news believed—but not everyone. The priests, the temple guard and the Sadducees weren't very happy, especially when Peter healed the lame beggar in the temple courts in Jesus' name (and then had a few pointed words to say about how the people of Israel had treated Jesus!). They were the ones who seized Peter and John and threw them into jail. They went off to prison right in the middle of all the joy; people were still coming to faith and the numbers growing as the doors slammed shut on those who'd delivered the message of hope.

We were frightened for them. We were beginning to realise they were seen as a serious threat. What might the authorities do to them?

The next day, the rulers, the elders and the teachers of the law, including the high priest and members of his family, questioned Peter and John. It was all so very sad, as well as scary. These men—these elders and teachers and rulers—are our leaders, our authority figures. They know the word of God inside out; yet on this day they could not see what was plain to all. Jesus had risen and it was in his name that people were being healed and saved. But they just couldn't accept it.

In fact, they must have been in a state of total confusion. They could see the remarkable things happening around them. They couldn't deny the miracles that were happening before their eyes. The lame beggar who'd been healed the previous day was standing right in front of them! They also knew that Peter and John were just unschooled, ordinary people. (The word was out that they used to be Galilean fishermen!) The rulers and teachers knew Peter and John had been with Jesus, and they could see that many were praising God for what had been happening.

What could they do to keep this 'thing' from spreading any further?

They found a solution—or so they thought. They told Peter and John to keep their mouths shut, threatened them, and set them free. As if! Clearly they just didn't get it. No-one could keep this news a secret! No threats that they could make were going to stop Peter and John from talking about what they had seen and heard, or from speaking and teaching in the name of Jesus!

So Peter and John came back to us, the believers gathered in Jerusalem, and told us what the chief priests and elders had said. We were so relieved to have them back among us, but we knew that trouble could easily erupt again—because, of course, they weren't going to keep their mouths shut! All we could do was lift our voices to God in prayer.

We prayed: "Sovereign Lord, you made it all—everything we see. And Lord, you spoke through King David. You told us about what would happen to your anointed one. And Lord, when Herod and Pontius Pilate met together with the Gentiles and the people of Israel in this city to conspire against Jesus, they all did what you had decided would happen long before."

Even amid all the chaos and opposition and threat, we knew that God was in control: all that was going on was happening just as he had intended. And we knew we could rely on him in the face of the rulers' threats. So we poured out our dependence on him in our prayers: "Consider their threats and enable your servants to speak your word with great boldness. Stretch out your hand to heal and perform signs and wonders through the name of your holy servant Jesus."

And that's when the earth shook. It was like a sign that God had heard us. Now, having been filled with God's Spirit on that day, we all speak the word of God boldly.

And we have been faithful in prayer ever since.

Bible study

Reflection/discussion points

- In times of human tragedy and loss, it is common for people to light candles in their grief (e.g. the news often shows people keeping vigil with candles lit in memory of someone who has died). What do you think drives this practice?

- Why are Christians called to pray?

Pray that this study would help you to hear the word of God and respond to it in a way that is pleasing to him.

Read Psalm 34

1. This is a psalm of King David in which he praises the Lord and calls on him with requests. Based on this psalm, who can petition the Lord?

2. What might keep God from listening to our prayers?

3. If God listens to "the righteous" (v 15) but his face is "against those who do evil" (v 16), how then can an unbeliever pray a prayer of repentance?

4. This psalm expresses the way Israel can relate to God. Given that we are not part of the Old Testament nation of Israel, what difference does Jesus make?

Read Ephesians 2:11-16 and then Hebrews 4:14-16

5. Jew and Gentile are now reconciled to God through the cross. What implications do the life and death of Jesus have for the believer's prayer life?

6. What implications do the life and death of Jesus have for the unbeliever when/if they pray?

Read Philippians 4:4-7

7. These are some of Paul's parting words to God's people in Philippi. What does Paul command in these verses?

8. What do these verses say about *why* we should pray? What do they say about *how* we should pray?

9. Will God always answer our prayers?

Implications

- Why do Christians today often struggle to pray?

- In the face of suffering or tragedy, is prayer helpful?

- What practices or routines can you put in place to encourage and promote your spiritual discipline of prayer?

Suggestions for prayer

Be creative (if in a group):

- Give everyone three different coloured slips of paper. On the first colour, ask everyone to write down one praise point; on the second colour, ask everyone to write down a prayer point for something or someone at church; and on the third colour, ask everyone to write down a prayer point for something or someone around the world.
- Put all the slips together and mix them up.
- Get everyone to draw out three random slips of paper (regardless of colour).

- Ask everyone in turn to pray a quick, one-sentence prayer for each of the slips in their hands; go around the group three times.
- Take your three slips home with you and pray for the three things/people listed on three different days in the coming week.

The struggle and privilege of prayer

Has your prayer life ever sounded like this?

Dear Lord and Father,

Help me now to come before your word and hear your voice. Help me—*oh wait, I forgot to lock the car!*

Sorry God, just got distracted. I pray that you would open my mind and heart and—*I must remember to pick up some milk on the way home. Should I go out after church this week? It will be a busy week—maybe I should get home and get to bed instead.*

Whoops, get back to praying; sorry God. Where was I? Something about opening my mind ... oh that's right, I pray that you will help me to obey what you want me to obey—*I wonder if I will see Steve after church*—oh, not now! God, help me to focus and I pray ... I can't remember—well ...

In Jesus' name, Amen.

Is it just me, or are there times when you struggle to pray? Christians know they should pray, and it is wonderful to have an open line to the only God of the universe, yet that doesn't mean Christians always find it easy. Sadly, we often fail in the area of prayer, and it can lead to disillusionment and lack of discipline in this important area of the Christian life.

In this chapter, we'll look at the essential and practical Christian topic of prayer.

What is prayer?

Prayer is when you talk to God. It could be to praise him, it could be to thank him, it could be to confess to him, or it could be to ask him for help. Prayer can be out loud, in our minds, in public or in private. Prayer can be simply between the pray-er and God or be something that several people do as they talk to God together.

Prayer is fundamentally an expression of relationship. It shows that Christians enjoy open access to God. It is one of the blessings that Christ won for us! Without Jesus dying on our behalf—without Jesus opening up a way to bring us to God—prayer would be pointless.

Prayer is a communal activity in that a Christian prays to the Father, with the Holy Spirit interceding, in the name of the Lord Jesus. It is not as if the Father, Spirit and Son need us to pray to them. What they choose to do to save or to act in the world is entirely up to them. Yet in prayer, we join God at his table—a graciously bestowed and wonderful privilege.

Prayer does not cost us anything; it is something anyone can do; and it can happen anywhere, no matter how good or bad the circumstance prompting the prayer might be!

If you can remember a time when you 'became a Christian', you'll know that it would have been prayer that was your first act of faith. You would have asked God to be the Lord of your life. And without wanting to be too morbid, prayer may indeed also be your last act of faith as you cast your fears on God as Lord at the end of your life.

Prayer in the Bible

The Bible is very comfortable with the idea that you can talk to God. Depending on the Bible version you look at, prayer is referenced over 650 times!

As you work through the Old Testament there is a lot said about prayer. The people of God are not called to pray; they just do. Abraham and Isaac prayed for children (Gen 20:17, 25:21). Jacob prayed that he would be saved from his angry brother (Gen 32:11). Moses sang in prayer to the Lord once Israel was delivered through the Red Sea (Exod 15:1-18). Moses, in fact, became a model of prayer as he interceded repeatedly for Israel while they travelled towards the promised land.[2]

David prayed when he was undecided about attacking the Philistines (1 Sam 23:1-4). Solomon prayed as he dedicated the temple to the Lord (1 Kgs 8:22-54). Throughout Psalms and Chronicles there are numerous examples of both David and Solomon calling out to God in prayer, praise or lament. And the list goes on.

There are wonderful examples in Scripture of God's Old Testament people talking to God in prayer. Nothing seemed to be too great or too hard for God. Things that seemed impossible and out of reach were given. Victories over nations and armies, and control over fire, wind, earth and water were all made possible—and why? Because the people of God asked of God, and he listened and mercifully answered their prayers.

Here is a thought to ponder. Not every spiritual practice carries over from the Old Testament into the New Testament. The writer to the Hebrews spends a lot of time

2   See Exod 17:4, 32:11-13, 33:12-23; Num 11:2, 11-15, 21-22; 12:13; 14:13-19.

helping the reader to understand what has changed. For example, circumcision, the mark of Israel, was present in the Old Testament but lost its significance as the mark of a believer in the New Testament church. The sacrificial system of the old covenant was replaced by the new covenant in the one true and lasting sacrifice of Jesus. But prayer is one discipline that runs from the Old Testament right through into the New Testament and on until today. Why? Because Jesus considered that prayer was important and necessary.

As we move into the New Testament we meet the master pray-er!

Consider some of the key moments in Jesus' life.

Right at the beginning of his ministry, after he has announced himself to the world by healing the sick and demon possessed and as the crowds gather, he goes off to a solitary place to pray (Mark 1:35; Luke 5:16).

In choosing his disciples, he prays (all night) and then appoints the twelve (Luke 6:12-16).

In the garden of Gethsemane, just before his arrest, he prays:

- for *himself*—"Father, if you are willing, take this cup from me; yet not my will, but yours be done" (Luke 22:42; cf. Matt 26:42; Mark 14:36)
- for his *disciples*—"My prayer is … that you protect them from the evil one" (John 17:15)
- for *all believers*—"I pray also for those who will believe in me … that all of them may be one" (John 17:20-21).

And on the cross as he is dying, Jesus cries out and prays, "Father, forgive them, for they do not know what they are doing" (Luke 23:34).

These prayers are extraordinary, not just because of the extreme humility and selflessness demonstrated, but because of the circumstances that surrounded Jesus at the times at which he prayed these prayers. Jesus is the model of faithfulness in prayer.

It is no wonder that the disciples led the church in prayer. They were taught by the best. We see in Acts that the early church learned what Jesus taught them because they held to the importance of meeting together to listen to the apostles' teaching, of fellowship, of the breaking of bread together and of prayer (Acts 2:42). There are numerous other examples of the apostles and believers at large in prayer in the book of Acts (Acts 4:23-31 is just one example).

The apostle Peter teaches that the ears of the Lord are attentive to the prayers of the righteous (1 Pet 3:12). James, the brother of Jesus, in his letter calls on any believer who is in trouble to pray (Jas 5:13).

The apostle Paul was obviously a big fan of prayer!

In Philippians, he reminds the church that in faith there is no need to be anxious about anything, but in everything, by prayer and petition, with thanksgiving they should present their requests to God (Philippians 4:6, as we saw in the Bible study above).

In Romans, Paul exhorts the church to "be joyful in hope, patient in affliction, faithful in prayer" (Rom 12:12).

To the Corinthians, he says not to even let sex with your spouse prevent you from being devoted to prayer (1 Cor 7:5).

He instructs the Ephesians to "pray in the Spirit on all occasions with all kinds of prayers and requests" (Eph 6:18).

In his letter to the Colossians, Paul just plainly states, "Devote yourselves to prayer" (Col 4:2).

It seems clear in the testimony of Scripture that prayer is a good thing, and a directive for all disciples saved in faith.

Misunderstanding prayer

If a Christian misunderstands either the nature or the urgency of prayer then it will have an impact on the way that they pray.

You will fail to understand the *nature* of prayer if you don't recognize that when you are praying, God is actually listening.

The result: prayer is going to feel pointless or, at best, unnatural.

Furthermore, if you pray expecting that God will always give you what you ask for (your will, not his), then prayer will become more of a wish list.

The result: in time, you will stop praying when it appears that God does not answer all your prayers.

You will fail to understand the *urgency* of prayer if you don't recognize how necessary and important to God it is that you pray.

The result: prayer will get crowded out (with the many other things that demand your attention) or taken for granted (especially if you have not recognized answered prayers) or devalued because you will start to think that you can handle things yourself (and often the burdens we have are not severe enough to make us think otherwise).

Let me tell you—both the devil and the world want you to misunderstand prayer because they think they know what is best for you. Whatever our struggles with prayer, the way to handle these struggles is not to sink into guilt or to give up, but to pause and think again about the privilege of being able to talk to God, who wants to give you what is best.

Prayer in Western society

So why do we, today, find prayer so difficult? I suspect the answer to this question will differ between the Western world and the Eastern world.

By world standards, I live in an affluent Western country (I suspect many reading this do as well). This impacts my prayer life! One danger is that I can become cynical. Let me explain.

There are many good things that individuals and our society at large have had to work very hard to accomplish. Those are things we like to enjoy—new buildings, breakthroughs in medical science, sporting successes, the ability to purchase a new home, promotions at work, good grades at school or college or university … and on it goes. With every success comes the 'pat on the back'! This reinforces the idea that we are good; that we can accomplish anything that we put our minds to; that we are self-sufficient. From a Western (and secular) point of view, what role is God allowed to have in that success? Usually a small one, if any role at all.

Yet, as good as things get, there are still the bad things that confront our world: sickness, disappointment, failure, unemployment, breakdown in relationship, and eventually death. If we were consistent as a society, wanting to take *all* credit, we would look at the bad things and work out what we did wrong. But that is not generally the case. It is often God who gets the blame for any of the bad things that occur, while we as a society pat ourselves on the back for the good things. The result: we are caused to question the goodness of God.

Here is where cynicism takes root.

Driving our Western cynicism is the relentless pursuit of perfectionism—that drive to have the perfect relationship, be in the perfect job, have the perfect family, enjoy the perfect social life, groom the perfect body, and attend the perfect school or university. Yet, despite every effort, we cannot call all the shots. We cannot control all that happens. And so, at some point, we come to realize how powerless we really are and it leaves us with a critical or disappointed spirit and an unhealthy cynicism about our world or about God.

As a Christian living in the Western world, I am at risk of an unhealthy cynicism. It is driven by my desire to be independent and in control. In this context, prayer doesn't work! Prayer is pointless, as if we are talking to the wind.

Thankfully, the Bible takes a different view. The prayers in the Bible engage with evil, they acknowledge both the good and the bad, and they express dependence upon God, who hears and cares and answers. And the people praying in the Bible don't give up on life; they don't expect "No" as the answer; they don't assume they have the final say and can ultimately determine what is right or wrong. The people praying in the Bible call upon a Father who can save them, and who, while remaining just, is loving and exercises his power for the good of all who trust him.

For close to two decades, I have been involved in sending Australian church teams to India to teach Bible subjects to pastors and key leaders. It is a ministry that brings the Christian West to the Christian East!

When Christians pray in India, they are free of many of

the Western trappings that I experience in Australia. One of the Australian team leaders wrote to me in 2015 about the way he saw Christians praying in India:

> Over chai at afternoon tea, a number of pastors approach me asking for prayer. Prayer for their children. Prayer for their ministry. Prayer for themselves and their own struggles. What a privilege to share with one another and bring our needs before our heavenly Father. Yet again I am rebuked by the urgency and immediacy with which my Indian brothers and sisters pray. Prayer isn't an afterthought. Prayer is never Plan B. Prayer is their first resort. It is their instinct and reflex. I'm reminded each time I come to India that the Western self-reliance ingrained in my DNA robs me of the intimacy of prayer. It foolishly lulls me into thinking I'm strong when in reality I'm helplessly weak. Oh Lord, rid me of my self-reliance and bring me to my knees in heartfelt, honest, dependent prayer.

The faithfulness in prayer displayed by those brothers and sisters in India bears a closer resemblance to the way the Bible talks about prayer than what is experienced by many Western Christians.

The impossible self-reliant perfectionism of many Western countries breeds an unhealthy cynicism—and one casualty of this is prayer. Cynicism looks in the wrong direction. It looks for the cracks in faith instead of looking at Jesus. We should not give up on prayer just because our world thinks it has all the answers. And prayer should not be the last resort when our world realizes that it *doesn't* have all the answers. The more self-reliant we think we are, the less we will recognize the need and the privilege it is to be able to call upon God in prayer.

Praying the Lord's way

So how do we pray? As we come to thinking about how to pray, our desire is often to jump quickly to tips and techniques—partly because we struggle and we know we need practical help! We will get there later in the chapter. But let us first start where Jesus starts: by looking at our deeper motivations and attitudes.

When Jesus taught his disciples to pray, he didn't start with a raft of techniques, but by addressing their hearts. His instruction in Matthew 6 came in the middle of a sermon, called the "Sermon on the Mount" (hardly surprising, as Jesus often withdrew to a mountain to pray). He began by expressing his concern that the disciples would conduct themselves in a way that was pleasing to the Lord as opposed to pleasing before people (v 1), and he offered three areas of concern: giving (vv 2-4), prayer (vv 5-15) and fasting (vv 16-18).

This is what he says about prayer:

> "And when you pray, do not be like the hypocrites, for they love to pray standing in the synagogues and on the street corners to be seen by others. Truly I tell you, they have received their reward in full. But when you pray, go into your room, close the door and pray to your Father, who is unseen. Then your Father, who sees what is done in secret, will reward you. And when you pray, do not keep on babbling like pagans, for they think they will be heard because of their many words. Do not be like them, for your Father knows what you need before you ask him.
>
> This, then, is how you should pray:
>
> > 'Our Father in heaven,
> > hallowed be your name,
> > your kingdom come,

your will be done,
> on earth as it is in heaven.

Give us today our daily bread.

And forgive us our debts,
> as we also have forgiven our debtors.

And lead us not into temptation,
> but deliver us from the evil one.'

For if you forgive other people when they sin against you, your heavenly Father will also forgive you. But if you do not forgive others their sins, your Father will not forgive your sins." (Matt 6:5-15)

The contrast in the passage is between the hypocrite or pagan (who stands in high places to be seen, or who babbles and uses many words) and the righteous one (who prays privately, not for esteem, and presumably not using babbling words to prop up the prayer).

Christians should pray like the righteous one! So, when you pray, don't pray like a hypocrite looking for credit from people. Instead, pray like a child asking something of his or her father. Like any good father, God knows what you need and, if it is best, will give it to you.

What Jesus offers his disciples is a prayer that we have come to know as the 'Lord's Prayer'. It is not a formula that must be followed, but it does show us all we need to know about who God is, about who we are before God, and about our dependence on him in prayer.

Here is a breakdown of how Jesus teaches his disciples to pray.

Our Father in heaven

He calls on God as provider and as the one over all. This means you can be less concerned with the mechanics of your prayer and recognize that when you are praying you are simply talking to God, your Father.

Hallowed be your name

God has the name before all names. He is set apart for honour in a way that no other deserves, so give him the esteem and credit that is due to him.

Your kingdom come

You don't have a kingdom unless you are a king, and this recognizes God in his rightful place as the majestic ruler and owner of all.

Your will be done on earth as it is in heaven

How terrific it is to have all authority. This recognizes God as the one whose will does matter most, be it on earth or in the heavens. He is over all. In prayer, we pray to God—not to one another, not to ourselves, but to the one who can answer even our audacious and seemingly impossible prayers. Yet note that we are not praying that God would change his will to match ours. We are praying that we might honour and accept his will over ours.

Give us today our daily bread

Ask for what is necessary and know that it is God who provides. The picture of "daily bread" is a reminder of Israel's reliance upon God as they travelled through the desert, totally dependent upon God to provide them with food to eat (quail and manna) and water to drink (from the rock)— see Exodus 16-17.

Forgive us our debts (or sins)

What debt do we owe? Regardless, it is God who can cancel that debt. To pray this shows a humility and willingness to declare our unrighteousness, and at the same time acknowledge and accept God's forgiveness.

As we also have forgiven our debtors (or those who have sinned against us)

This presumes that the pray-er has indeed forgiven those who have sinned against them. This call for forgiveness is elaborated on in verses 14-15:

> "For if you forgive other people when they sin against you, your heavenly Father will also forgive you. But if you do not forgive others their sins, your Father will not forgive your sins."

Forgiveness is the driving reality of prayer. If Christians can be forgiven by the one who knows all, then the person who is a Christian should also be forgiving others. In this sense, prayer mirrors the gospel. In the gospel, the Father takes us as we are because Jesus gives his gift of salvation (as we saw in chapter 1, 'Saved by grace'). In prayer, the Father receives us as we are because Jesus has given us the gift of his help.

And lead us not into temptation

Temptation is not sin, but its risk is that it will lead to sin, so we ask God to lead us away from that danger.

But deliver us from the evil one

Every person will encounter the evil that is in the world, and this prayer particularly acknowledges the greatest threat to the one who is righteous—the evil one, the devil.

. . .

What a blessing to be taught how to pray; to be given a direct line to our Father in heaven; to know that we can ask, talk, plead, cry out, praise him, confess to him—and no matter what, he will hear. And what a comfort it is to know that from the best of circumstances to the very worst situations, prayer is something that a Christian can do. You don't have to be able to speak, hear, see or move—and yet you can still pray.

We may look at the inadequacy of our praying and feel the temptation to give up. But God looks at the adequacy of his Son and delights in our sloppy, meandering prayers, as we come to him as Father.

Tips for prayer

Prayer is essential, and so, as promised, here are some tips and suggestions to help you essentially pray:

1. Aim to be consistent, intentional and regular in prayer

Everyone is different in their pattern of prayer (e.g. hourly, daily, weekly), but if you rarely pray or have no form or pattern it is unlikely that you will be consistent, intentional or regular in prayer.

Suggestion: You might find that using some form of prayer journal (physical or electronic) to record what you pray can help (and it has the added advantage of allowing you to look back at what you have prayed and how God has answered).

2. Use Scripture to inform your prayers

Praying in response to a Bible passage is a helpful way to allow God's word to shape your prayer life (and for that reason, many put their Bible and prayer time together—a 'personal devotion'). There are wonderful prayers in both the Old and New Testaments which can be prayed as if they were your own prayers (e.g. 1 Chron 29:10-13; Psalms 43, 145; Acts 4:24-30; Rom 11:33-36; Phil 1:9-11).

Suggestion: Use liturgical prayers like the formal prayers that may be used in your church, or set prayers like the Lord's Prayer (Matt 6:9-15; Luke 11:2-4), which can be helpful because they cover those matters that the Lord has said he is most concerned about.

3. Pray with purpose

JC Ryle (a 19th-century preacher and writer) encouraged the person of faith to pray reverently and humbly before the Lord, spiritually (relying on the Spirit to intercede), regularly (as part of the business of life), perseveringly, earnestly, faithfully, boldly and fully, particularly and thankfully.[3] What he is suggesting is that you give yourself over deeply in prayer.

Suggestions:

(a) When you pray, don't just look inward to your own concerns—pray *up* (praising and calling upon God) and *out* (praying for those around you, including those who don't know Jesus).

---

3   JC Ryle, *A Call to Prayer*, American Tract Society, 1836.

(b) Pray regularly with others. Praying with others can be a wonderful privilege, and opportunities abound (at least in countries where it is not outlawed): with your spouse or a good friend, with the family, in 'prayer triplets', at church prayer meetings, in Bible study groups, and more.

4. Set aside a time or marker for prayer

We can be helped by forming habits. Aim to put in place helpful, regular habits around when you pray. For example, it could be the first thing you do when you rise in the morning, following lunch (whenever that might be), in the shower, before you watch any TV, and so on. You may be the kind of person who works well by setting a calendar reminder.

Suggestion: Use technology to help prompt prayer—a prayer app (e.g. PrayerMate or Echo) or a recurring calendar entry with message prompts can be very helpful in setting time markers for prayer.

5. Pray as opportunity arises

See or hear a concern and use it as a prompt to immediately pray. Be spontaneous. Instead of saying that you *will* pray for something, just pray, then and there.

Suggestions: Use birthdays as a prompt for prayer. Those on Facebook get a reminder each day of whose birthday it is—a great reminder to pray for your 'friends'! Pray in response to the lead story on your newsfeed each day.

6. Organize your prayers

Develop a system that prompts you to pray for things that are godly concerns and personal concerns.

Suggestions:

(a) Use a 31-day calendar and write onto each day what/who you are praying for—then pray for those things on the appointed day each month (keep a copy in your Bible or at the location where you most regularly pray).

(b) Use a prayer card system: write down whatever prayer concern you have on a card, then cycle through the cards a few at a time when you pray—this is an easy way to add and remove prayer concerns as they arise or resolve.

• • •

Whatever you do—pray! And always remember that "the eyes of the Lord are on the righteous and his ears are attentive to their prayer" (1 Peter 3:12, quoting Psalm 34:15).

Perhaps now would be a good time to pray!

What's best next?

• What aspects of your thinking and your behaviour should be changed as a result of reflecting on this 'essential' Christian quality?

• What step can you take this week to make that change?

Pray about it.

4. BOLD IN WITNESS

The world says: Watch yourself! Don't say anything we deem intolerant or confronting, or you'll be 'cancelled'.

But God says: Make Jesus famous, so that others will know how important it is that Jesus died for them.

A voice from Acts: "Who can I talk to next?"

Inspired by Acts 17:16-34

I'd been waiting in Athens for some time, and the more time I spent here, the more distressed I had become.

It's a wonderful city in so many ways; a magnificent tribute to human creativity and endeavour. There's the massive harbour of Piraeus, with trading boats sailing in from all corners of the world. There's the Temple of Zeus, with its imposing columns reaching up to the sky-high ceiling, and statues everywhere, one to this god and another to that god. They do religion very thoroughly here!

At the entrance to the city stands the grand Hadrian's

Arch. On one side of the arch the city is dedicated to Emperor Hadrian; but on the other side, the dedication is to the mythical King Theseus. (There's politics behind everything, and this city is no exception!) And there's the huge, two-tiered covered colonnade called the Stoa of Attalus, the largest marketplace around—making this city a centre of culture and fashion.

I was told when I arrived here that the Epicurean and Stoic philosophers sit day by day in the marketplace and argue about ideas. It's a culture pervaded by ideas and idealism. And all of this takes place in the shadow of the Acropolis. Many Greek cities have some kind of citadel constructed on a hill overlooking the city, but none is as formidable or as famous as the Parthenon perched high above Athens—making this a city of power, not to mention a tourism gold mine.

So while I waited for Timothy and Silas to join me, I occupied myself well in this great city of ideas and idols. I started talking with people in the synagogue first, and talked to some people in the marketplace, but I very quickly realised that the ones who really wanted to hear from me (and debate with me) were the philosophers. They took me with them to the Areopagus, to a meeting of the governing body of the city.

As I said before, I had begun to feel distressed as I spent time in this city. The people were so keen to worship, but the object of their worship was idols. And as I began to engage in conversations with people, I was distressed not because of the way I was treated, but because of the way that the people in this city regarded our Lord.

You see, I had been preaching the good news about Jesus and his resurrection, but the people of the city thought that

I was advocating for a foreign god—perhaps just another god like their many idols. But at least the philosophers were interested enough to ask me about what they called "this new teaching" and the "strange ideas" I was bringing to their ears (although I suspect, at that point, they were just seeking out a new subject about which they could postulate—like I said, they do love discussing the latest ideas!).

So here I was, Paul, a servant of Christ Jesus, set apart for the gospel of God, standing before a group of strangers at the Areopagus. Ever since my Lord appeared to me and called me to be his witness, I had sought and found opportunities to testify about him. Up until now, as I had travelled about telling others about Jesus I had always started in the synagogue with the Jews and then moved on to appeal to the Gentiles—but this time I was far from the synagogue, and all of those standing before me were Gentiles.

How was I to begin explaining the one true God to them when they had little or no knowledge of his existence or the history of his people? How could I introduce them to Jesus?

I began: "People of Athens! I see that in every way you are very religious." I described what I had seen around their great city—the statues, the monuments, the objects of worship. It was clear to me that while they were very religious, they were also lost. It was all in vain—they had no idea who to worship! I had rarely felt so sad. They needed to be shown the truth.

I remembered that I had seen an altar inscribed 'To AN UNKNOWN GOD'! I had an idea—I'd use this unknown 'idol' to testify about Jesus.

I started with this 'unknown god', saying that the word 'unknown' showed that they themselves realized that they were ignorant of the very thing they worshipped. But they obviously thought highly of the 'gods', so I taught them about the sovereign and provident nature of the *true* God: it was God who made all, the heavens and the earth, and it's God who gives life to all people. I told them that God is not limited to the many temples in their city; he is not served or provided for by the people of Athens; he doesn't need anything, as he created it all in the first place! All nations, including the people of Athens, were made so that all would seek him out and reach out to him.

I knew my hearers were intelligent people. If ever there was a city that should be able to understand the importance of an all-sovereign and generous God, it was Athens! I let them know that I could see how thoughtful and perceptive they were, and how much they already understood, saying, "As some of your own poets have said, 'We are his offspring'".

So far so good.

Next, I described God's judgement. This was not such a popular topic! First I had to bring up the topic of their idol worship. I said, "Since we are God's offspring, we should not think that the divine being is like gold or silver or stone—an image made by human design and skill". I said that in the past God had overlooked the ignorance of people who put their faith in such things, but now God was asking all people to repent.

This seemed to challenge my listeners a bit. They frowned and shifted uneasily, whispering sideways and casting doubtful, even hostile, looks and gestures in my direction. But this was just what I'd hoped. Now that they knew about the one true God, they needed to repent—to turn away from the mistakes we all make and the liberties we all take when we ignore what God actually asks of us. They couldn't have understood the need for this before; but now they needed to. They needed to realize that God wanted them to turn back to him.

And then I introduced them to Jesus.

Even if nothing else was sinking in yet, at the very least I needed to share the news of Jesus with them.

"There is a day coming", I said, "when the man God has appointed as judge will judge the world with justice and set all things right". Everyone likes the idea of true justice; the idea of a day when right will be shown to be right and wrong will be shown to be wrong. I explained to them that this judge appointed by God is Jesus, and that we know this because God raised Jesus from death to life. I told them that he can be the judge of both the living and the dead—because he is the only one who has lived after death.

Well, talking about Jesus' resurrection caused an interesting response—as it always does! The gathered crowd murmured to each other. I could see some shaking their heads, some huddled in intense conversation, and some walking away. Some openly sneered. Some spoke to me, wanting to arrange a time to hear more. And some believed, then and there.

They believed because I witnessed to them of Jesus' death and resurrection. This is what Jesus commissioned me to do—be his witness. It doesn't mean everyone will accept what I say, but it does mean that those who want to hear more can ask, and that some of those who hear will believe.

Right: who can I talk to next?

Bible study

Reflection/discussion points

- What is an evangelist?

- The Bible talks about both "witnesses" and "eyewitnesses". Is there an important difference?

Pray that this study would help you to hear the word of God and respond to it in a way that is pleasing to him.

Note: Be ready for some Bible surfing! The Bible has a lot to say about this topic, so we need to see the development in the scope of "witness" from Israel (God's old covenant people) through to all nations (under God's new covenant).

Suggestion: Create a 'witness timeline', plotting each of the verses you read to show the development of these ideas.

Read Psalm 96

1. The psalmist calls "all the earth" (v 1) to sing to the Lord. What should they sing and proclaim and declare? Why?

2. How does Psalm 96 bring together both the salvation and the judgement of the Lord?

Read Matthew 1:18-21

3. What do we learn about what Jesus came to do? Who specifically will he save?

4. Notice how both salvation and judgement are brought together in Jesus. How does this fulfil what Psalm 96 announced?

Read Matthew 10:5-10 and Luke 10:1-12

5. In each of these passages, to whom does Jesus send his disciples?

6. In each case, what message does he instruct them to proclaim?

7. In each case, what do you think this message means?

Note: When Jesus enters Jerusalem days before his death, his first stop is the Jewish temple (Matt 21:10-13). The opposition he faces begins with the chief priests and the teachers of the law (Matt 21:15) and continues in the chapters that follow, through to his trial (finishing at Matt 27:26). The last question Jesus answers comes from Pilate: "Are you the king of the Jews?" Jesus' answer is simple: "You have said so" (Matt 27:11). He is crucified. Three days later he rises from the dead.

Read Matthew 28:16-20

8. To whom does Jesus now send the disciples? What has changed since he sent his disciples out in Matthew 10 and Luke 10 (see above)?

9. On what basis does Jesus send them?

10. What is the message that the disciples are to take?

11. What promise does Jesus make to his disciples?

Read Acts 1:6-8

12. This was the last time Jesus met with his disciples before being taken up into heaven. What did the disciples expect Jesus to do?

13. What did Jesus tell them would happen?

What follows in the book of Acts is a record of the gospel going out from Jerusalem into all Judea and Samaria, en route to the ends of the earth (the Gentile nations). Have a quick look through Acts at the gospel's progress, noticing especially what is said in the following verses: Acts 2:41, 2:47, 6:7, 9:31, 12:24, 13:49, 16:5, 19:20, 28:31.

Read Revelation 7:9-10

14. In this vision of what is to come, who will be present? Whom will they be standing before?

15. What new song will they be singing? How is it like the song of Psalm 96? How is it different?

Implications

- What should being a "witness" of Christ look like today—in our families, in our workplaces, in our places of study, and in our church?

- If we recognise that Jesus calls all disciples, including those who follow him today, to be his "witnesses", what would be an inappropriate or wrong way for a Christian to view evangelism (telling others about Christ)?

Suggestions for prayer

- Give thanks for the person or people who first told you the good news about Jesus.
- Pray for opportunities to share what you know about Jesus, and that you would make the most of every opportunity.
- Pray for your church, that together you might be bold in witness.

Celebrity Jesus?

I love celebrity. I mean real celebrity.

A celebrity is publicly known for something distinctive—something that others can look at, write about or admire. A celebrity is someone whom others want to follow, or know, or be like. Maybe they can move faster, or jump further, or climb higher, or dive deeper, or hit harder. Maybe they can sing more loudly, or act more convincingly, or dance more expertly, or write more creatively, or speak more persuasively, or make people laugh more hysterically. Maybe they can make more money, or invent more things, or manage more people. There are many reasons why someone becomes famous and stands out in a culture.

When we follow celebrity, there is always a cost. It may be our time, money or energy. When the entertainer arrives on our shores, we pay (sometimes exorbitant amounts of money!) to go and see them. When our favourite team plays our favourite sport we dress up in the team colours (regardless of how ridiculous we might look) and head out to support them. When a royal arrives we line the streets (well, some of us do) and cheer. We read about celebrities. We buy products or services promoted by celebrities. And then when they die, we collectively mourn those celebrities.

Yet celebrities come and go. For so many, their star shines for a while, and then when the talent or reason that got them the attention in the first place loses its appeal, the celebrity fades from view. The mark of a *genuine* celebrity is that they continue across the years to gain attention and be appreciated by the wider public (even if that means being ridiculed at the same time). Often, these celebrities become known and loved for things that are secondary to why they first came to public attention. Genuine celebrity is rare.

Let me ask you a question: Would you say Jesus was a celebrity?

It seems like a crass way to talk about Jesus; worldly at best. But, for a moment, let us just think about Jesus the celebrity.

Jesus is known by others for something distinctive—he came to offer forgiveness of sins and life forever with God. He offers something that, frankly, no-one else can offer. People have looked at, have written about, and admire who he is and what he did. There are people who follow him and want to know about him and find out how they can do what he did. Over the centuries, he has gained attention and continued to be appreciated by the wider public. Yes, he has his critics (as celebrities tend to have), and it is not uncommon for people to look at Jesus and focus on things that seem to be secondary to what he claimed was most important— they see him now as only a good teacher, a miracle worker, a moral man, a radical, or a political manoeuvrer.

Yes, Jesus does fit the bill. In many ways Jesus is a celebrity. He is famous.

Yet there is something very un-celebrity-like about Jesus. His star shines not for his benefit, but for those he came to save. The benefit of following Jesus, despite the cost, is all for the one doing the following!

Taking our stand

The topic of this chapter is 'Bold in witness'. It is so named because boldness is what Jesus asked of his disciples. And "witness" is what Jesus' first disciples did—they bore witness to Jesus.

Yet note that *they* didn't make Jesus famous any more than they made him king, or ruler, or Christ, or Lord—for Jesus was all of those and more. Their efforts to make Jesus famous were the result of them obeying what Jesus had commanded them.

To be a *witness* means that you have seen, have heard, or know something that will be helpful for others as they make their own decisions as to the credibility of the matter about which you are giving testimony. For example, in most legal systems, evidence is given by either an *eyewitness* (someone who actually saw or heard firsthand) or an *expert witness* (someone who has qualified knowledge or experience in a particularly relevant field). As such, to *bear witness*, you must be willing to take the stand, to testify, to speak on behalf of the person or the event that you are bearing witness to. The aim is to provide enough reason or evidence for someone who is not a witness to ascertain the truth behind what you say.

Jesus appeared on many occasions to his disciples following his death, and before his final appearance he said:

> "This is what is written: The Messiah will suffer and rise from the dead on the third day, and repentance for the forgiveness of sins will be preached in his name to all nations, beginning at Jerusalem. You are witnesses of these things." (Luke 24:46-48)

It is not every day that a dead person comes back to life! For that event to have credibility there would need to be evidence, and one of the best types of evidence is that of personal testimony and witness. The disciples, having been with Jesus for the best part of three years, had heard what he had taught, had seen what he could do, had listened as he explained Old Testament Scripture, had come to understand that he was indeed the Messiah, and had been mystified when Jesus had predicted his own death and resurrection. Theoretically, they should have been able to connect the dots better than anyone.

When those predicted events—his arrest, his suffering, his death and then, incredibly, his resurrection—happened, and happened just as Jesus said they would, the disciples found themselves in a unique position. What they knew was no longer theoretical. It was now historical fact. And they were the witnesses—both *eyewitnesses* and *expert witnesses*.

The *good news* about Jesus would only be *news* if it was told. And the good news about Jesus would only be known to be *good* if it was explained. The disciples had a job to do!

The Great Commission

Matthew's Gospel finishes with what is called the "Great Commission". Again, the resurrected Jesus stands before his disciples. He says:

> "All authority in heaven and on earth has been given to me. Therefore go and make disciples of all nations, baptizing them in the name of the Father and of the Son and of the Holy Spirit, and teaching them to obey everything I have commanded you. And surely I am with you always, to the very end of the age." (Matt 28:18-20)

Look at the instruction that Jesus gives: "Make disciples of all nations". This is a command that will not be fulfilled unless the disciples go out and address those of the nations. As they testify—as they proclaim the good news about Jesus—people will come to believe, and they are the ones who should be baptized and then instructed in how to live their lives. To make disciples, therefore, one must go, baptize into belief, and teach what it means to be a disciple. In giving them this commission, Jesus is instructing his disciples to go and do what he had first done with them. Just in case that job freaks them out (after all, it is rather daunting), Jesus finishes with a wonderful assurance—he tells them to go remembering that "I am with you always, to the very end of the age". Dwell on that promise for a moment. As you go and do what I have commanded (said Jesus), no matter how easy or hard you will find it—I will be with you, always.

In our secular world, we appoint. When a person gets a new job they accept an 'appointment', and that comes with the expectation that they will do the job for which they are hired. If they don't, then it is entirely appropriate that their appointment will be reviewed and they will be shown the door!

The Great Commission is like an appointment for Christians. Jesus effectively says to his disciples, "I have saved you, I have taught you, and now I have a job for you—my expectation is that you will go and do that job: make disciples of all nations". They did. We know they did, because we, today, are the disciples from those nations!

Believe and declare

The apostle Paul in Romans argues that a Christian cannot rightly call themselves a disciple unless they both *believe* and *declare* that "Jesus is Lord":

If you declare with your mouth, "Jesus is Lord," and believe in your heart that God raised him from the dead, you will be saved. For it is with your heart that you believe and are justified, and it is with your mouth that you profess your faith and are saved. As Scripture says, "Anyone who believes in him will never be put to shame." For there is no difference between Jew and Gentile—the same Lord is Lord of all and richly blesses all who call on him, for, "Everyone who calls on the name of the Lord will be saved."

How, then, can they call on the one they have not believed in? And how can they believe in the one of whom they have not heard? And how can they hear without someone preaching to them? And how can anyone preach unless they are sent? As it is written: "How beautiful are the feet of those who bring good news!" (Rom 10:9-15)

Paul's desire is to see people saved and he knows that salvation is found only in Jesus. So his argument here states that a person's salvation is on display when they are willing to *declare with their mouth* that "Jesus is Lord" and *believe in their heart* that God raised him from the dead.

There is an inward and outward expression of faith here—believe in your heart (the inward reality of being justified) and declare with your mouth (the outward expression of that justification).[4] This is the reality that drives mission. Paul models this in each of the evangelistic speeches he gives (as recorded in Acts)—in each, he testifies that God raised Jesus from the dead.

Pushing this a little further, can you see how this calls upon Christians to live out their faith publicly? It is not

---

4   As we noted in chapter 1, to be 'justified' is a way of saying that you are 'made right' before God.

sufficient to consider your faith in Jesus to be a private thing. What Paul is saying here is that if you believe that Jesus is Lord, then that is a belief that needs to be expressed publicly for others to hear. Christians should have Jesus on their lips.

Paul calls on the Roman Christians to go beyond the Jews (the Israel of his day) and to go to even the Gentiles to help everyone call on the name of the Lord. Your faith is on display as you bear witness to Jesus. Your testimony of Jesus should aim to help others call on the name of the Lord.

How does one *call* on Jesus if they don't *believe* in him? And how will one *believe* in Jesus if they have not *heard* about him? And how will one *hear* about Jesus without someone *telling* them? And how will that someone *tell others* about Jesus unless he or she is *sent* to do it?

Paul tells the followers of Christ to go and tell: for Jesus to be believed, witnesses need to be testifying about him. Someone must be sent, for someone to go, for someone to preach, for someone to hear, for someone to believe, and so call upon the Lord to be saved.

It is about making Jesus famous. Yet the benefit is for those who follow him.

So Christians—go and 'speak Jesus'.

Being bold in witness

Why is it that Christians are often reluctant to be bold in witness? For me, that is simple—it is often hard work, or I am too chicken, or I am too distracted, or I am …

I know the excuses, because I have used them all. I am a reluctant evangelist.

It is not uncommon for me to be standing on the sidelines of a soccer pitch watching my sons play football. Alongside me stand the other parents. A perfect opportunity to speak about Jesus?

I can tell you, it is easy to talk about our kids ("Your little Johnny seems to be playing well today!"), or the football (it is always the same two kids who have worked out that you are supposed to get the ball in the goal, while everyone else makes up the numbers!), or the weather (the ground we play on doubles as an Antarctic wind tunnel!). But it is not so easy to talk about things that really matter—like Jesus or what happens when we die.

Now, you could argue that watching the match on the sidelines of a freezing football field is neither the time nor the place to try and have a conversation about Jesus. It probably isn't. Early on in my years as a spectator, every time I mentioned Jesus the parent beside me either choked on their coffee or quickly found some reason to run over to the coach to offer advice!

All Christians will find themselves in situations where they stand among unbelievers—if not the football field, it will be the classroom, the workplace, the social club, the pub, the mothers' group, the retirement home ... the list goes on. None will be the ideal time or place to have a conversation about Jesus.

So, in the absence of the ideal situation to evangelize, and knowing that the football sideline is as good as any, what do I need to do to make the time and place right? I have a strategy, in which I take my lead from what Paul (and Timothy) said to the church in Colossae:

² Devote yourselves to prayer, being watchful and thankful. ³ And pray for us, too, that God may open a door for our message, so that we may proclaim the mystery of Christ, for which I am in chains. ⁴ Pray that I may proclaim it clearly, as I should. ⁵ Be wise in the way you act toward outsiders; make the most of every opportunity. ⁶ Let your conversation be always full of grace, seasoned with salt, so that you may know how to answer everyone. (Col 4:2-6)

Here's my strategy, then: four actions based on these verses from Colossians.

1. I pray

It's my secret weapon. If I am going to try and talk to people about God, then I should at least start by talking to God about people!

Here Paul brings both prayer and evangelism together. Those who are reconciled to God can talk to him in prayer. Yet those who are alienated from God won't talk to God. So Paul says to those who are, pray about those who are not! Pray particularly for opportunities to evangelize.

The concern driving this instruction to pray is that the "mystery of Christ" might be proclaimed (v 3). The "mystery of Christ" is just another way to talk about the gospel of Jesus Christ. It is a "mystery" to those who have not heard it or have not accepted it. Yet to Paul and to those who have accepted the gospel, there is no mystery, and so Paul's request is that a door would be opened and that the gospel would be proclaimed clearly.

Christians, pray for yourselves (to be alert and thankful), pray for Christians in general (and, at the very least, pray especially for those like Paul and Timothy who are

proclaiming Christ), and pray particularly for the clear proclamation of the gospel.[5]

There is nothing that should prevent me from standing on
the sidelines of the soccer pitch and praying. I can pray for
myself to be alert and ready and thankful for the opportunity
that sits before me to talk about Jesus. I can pray that a door
might be opened so that I can have a conversation about
Jesus with those standing near me. And I can pray that if I do
get the opportunity, I might proclaim the gospel clearly.

2. I draw in the allies

While it is possible that I am the only Christian parent standing on the sideline, it is often the case that others around
are also disciples of Christ. If that is the case, then drawing them into conversations that occur with those who are
not yet disciples is a helpful strategy. Why go it alone, when
there are others around who make up the numbers and
in fact can provide an affirming voice in any conversation
about matters of faith?

The fact that Paul asks the Colossian church to pray "for
us … so that we may proclaim" (v 3) gives an indication
that even Paul and Timothy could see the value of working
together in the way that they shared Jesus.

So call in the reinforcements, your allies in the cause of
the gospel. Intentionally work out ways to draw your not-
yet-Christian friends into collective conversations with your
Christian friends.

5   There is a theological question here that can divide Christians: Is every Christian
    called to be an evangelist, or only those Christians who are like Paul and
    Timothy? (For a discussion of this question, see appendix B, 'Is every Christian
    called to be an evangelist?') Even if you are of the opinion that evangelism is
    for other Christians to do, you should be praying for them.

3. I build relational connection

I want to grow a friendship with those whom I am trying to connect to Jesus. The time beside the football field is a very narrow window in which to gain any opportunity to talk with other parents, but it is enough of a window to set a Christian example and issue an invitation.

Again, look at what Paul says to the Colossian Christians: "Be wise in the way you act toward outsiders; make the most of every opportunity" (v 5). The way any Christian behaves is watched by the world. In part, that should happen because the Christian lives distinctively for Christ and not for the world, and so that discrepancy should be obvious. I take it that Paul's instruction here is to be wise so that the outsider can see and value the way a believer conducts himself or herself.

On the football sideline, my aim is to behave in a manner that is impressive before outsiders (e.g. not swearing, respecting the referee, keeping my cool, valuing the efforts of the players (on both teams), acknowledging the good plays that happen, and so on). My "wise" conduct is really a demonstration of the way Christ would like me to conduct myself.

Alongside that Christlike behaviour comes *opportunity*, and Paul says to make the most of those little opportunities with the hope that you will be able to get a foot in the door, which may lead to conversation or testimony about Jesus.

In an effort to build relational connection, I look for opportunities to invite others to something where the time and place would be right to talk about Jesus—and that may not be church in the first instance. For example, inviting my not-yet-Christian friends over for dinner (onto my turf), or to the pub, or to some good event that is put on somewhere will mean I get to know them (and they me) more deeply. While my intention is all relational, my aim is to create opportunities to speak about Jesus and then maybe, in time, invite them to church or to some evangelistic event or to read the Bible.

Bearing in mind the second point above, inviting Christian allies as well will mean that I am also helping to build relational connections with others so that my not-yet-Christian friend now has several different Christian voices surrounding them. When they come to see how awesome and 'normal' my Christian friends really are, they may also come to see that having faith in Jesus is not so strange or radical.

I take it that, given that the gospel invites people into a relationship with God through Jesus, my effort to build relationship will not only help create more opportunities, but also model the value of being Christian.

4. I talk about how Jesus intersects with life

As the firstborn of creation, Jesus is not far from most topics that matter in our world. He intersects with life on so many levels. As his witness, the Christian has a job: to be ready to talk about Jesus in a way that intersects with our lives, with the goal always being to share Jesus with others.

Although I am a Christian and those standing on the football sideline might not be, there is still much that we have in common—kids, football, weather, school, local news … These topics are a good place to start.

I talk about my kids and what I am doing to bring them up as people who follow Jesus and who know how to care for their friends. I talk about the football, and about playing hard and fair, and about treating others with respect because as Christians we are called to be honest and true before others. I talk about how God made the weather and how wonderful it is that he gives us a reminder that he is there every time that cold wind blows right through us! I talk about how well the school our kids attend teaches and shapes our kids, and how school values like honesty and perseverance were values that Jesus taught his disciples. I talk about events reported in the recent news that concern our city or suburb and look for a way to bring some gospel values and perspective to those events. What I am looking for is some way to talk about how Jesus intersects with our life.

Back to what Paul said to the Colossians: "Let your conversation be always full of grace, seasoned with salt, so that you may know how to answer everyone" (v 6). Paul's encouragement is to use words well. In conversation, the *manner* in which a Christian speaks should be gracious. Although the content of the gospel confronts many people and may draw objection, Christians want the manner in which they speak the gospel to draw no objection.

Further, the *character* of what is said in conversation should be distinctive. Salt is added to a meal to ensure that it is not bland, and as such the flavour stands out. When speaking, Christians should speak about Jesus distinctively, knowing that what he taught and how he lived was distinctive to the world around. It is appropriate to draw out the differences between Christian and secular worldviews.

Why be concerned about the *manner* and the *character* of the way you speak? So that as a Christian you know how to answer the gospel questions or objections that may arise in conversation. It is all part of being a reliable witness to Christ.

Why go to the effort to find ways to talk about Jesus? I can quite easily stand on the football sideline and keep to myself! I do it because I want to make Jesus famous. He is the Saviour of the world, and the world needs to hear about him to be saved.

Christians have been saved by Jesus, and he calls for them to bear witness to him, not so that he will benefit, but so that others will benefit. When people see Jesus for what is most distinctive about him, they may realize that he is more than what they may have first thought, and so turn and follow him.

Christian, live as an expert witness to Christ—and use words!

Practical tips

So what tips will help you to be bold in witness?

Pray

Talk to God and ask for opportunities to be a witness. Pray for those you might get to speak to. Pray about what you might say.

Be intentional

Write yourself a list of those around you whom you would like the opportunity to speak with. Think about what you might need to do to create the space and opportunity (under God) to talk with them about Jesus. They might be family members, work colleagues, teammates, school, college or university friends … the list goes on and on.

Learn how to explain the gospel

It will be difficult to proclaim the gospel clearly if you don't know what to say. So learn a simple way to explain the good news of Jesus.[6] There are tracts, Bible apps, videos and books that may help. The publisher of this book is well known for producing very helpful resources to help you explain the gospel. If you don't know what is most helpful, ask.

Learn how to give your testimony

Your story as a Christian involves Jesus because at some point you were confronted with the gospel (be it as far back as you can remember or a particular time when you accepted the gospel). For your Christian testimony to be helpful, it should be a testimony to Jesus using you as the example!

Be bold by the power of the Holy Spirit

Your job is to bear witness to Jesus; it is not to convert people. Conversion is the job of the Holy Spirit. Be bold in testifying about Jesus. Say something when normally you wouldn't. Work up the courage and give it a go! Recognize, however, that you are not responsible for how the person responds.

Serve those you are trying to reach

Most relationships grow when people care for one another. Christians should know how to do this better than anyone.

6 I use something I wrote called *JesusWORKS*—it is freely available at churchcentralonline.com/who-is-jesus.

Find ways to serve and help those you want to reach with the gospel (e.g. provide meals when they're sick, help out with moving or cleaning or building something, babysit, help them with a work task, share resources that will assist in study …).

Build relationship with those you are trying to reach

Sharing your life with someone will build relationship, so think of ways to invite the person you are trying to reach into your life (e.g. have them over for a meal and invite some Christian friends, invite them to join you in social or sporting activities …). This will take time, as all good friendships do.

Speak about Jesus

Look for and take opportunities, both individually (with those you come into contact with) and corporately (at your church evangelistic endeavours) to talk about Jesus. Help make Jesus famous! And when you speak about Jesus, know that you are carried along by the Holy Spirit.

Invite people to connect with Jesus

Don't fear asking those you are trying to reach to accept Jesus for themselves. You might ask them to read the Bible with you, pray with you, or come to church with you. The invitation won't come from them, so boldly issue the invitation to meet Jesus.

●　●　●

Remember, the goal of evangelism is always to share Jesus. And on the day when every knee bows, and every tongue confesses, and every eye sees—it will be Jesus who will be exalted. Until then, be bold in witness.

What's best next?

- What aspects of your thinking and your behaviour should be changed as a result of reflecting on this 'essential' Christian quality?

- What step can you take this week to make that change?

Pray about it.

5. RESILIENT IN SUFFERING

The world says: Don't worry, be happy; that should be your goal in life.

But God says: Persevere in the face of suffering and keep trusting me; your goals are not limited to this life.

A voice from Acts: "He was only trying to help."

Inspired by Acts 6-7

I can't believe it. They killed him.

He was only trying to help. He only said what he said to help them see what they couldn't or wouldn't. And instead of listening, they covered their eyes and yelled at the tops of their voices.

His name was Stephen. His job was to care for the widows—to care for me. Actually, if the truth be told, it wasn't his job at all. Under Jewish law it was the synagogue leaders who were supposed to be looking after the vulnerable and the poor. Ha! That wasn't happening. They were too busy making up laws and trying to enforce them on everyone else.

I had been connected to this group who were preaching the word about a guy called Jesus. There was something special in what they were saying; and, more than that, their words were backed up with actions—because they, the people who followed Jesus, were the ones making sure people like me were not being overlooked and left to starve.

But for some reason, the things that the people in this group were doing seemed to bother the authorities. They accused Stephen of speaking words of blasphemy against Moses and against God. I never heard him do any such thing! All he ever did was help others, by distributing food, and through other amazing things I've heard people talk about—signs and wonders, I suppose you'd call them. He never hurt anyone!

Anyway, some of those who didn't like what he was doing stirred up the people and the elders and the teachers. They took him before the council and some people stood up and suggested that he was speaking against the temple and against the law. More lies!

It got out of hand. All the bigwigs had turned up—the high priest and the teachers of the law. And Stephen stood up and tried to explain where they had got it all wrong. I'm not sure they were listening very well, though. From what I've heard, it looked like they'd already made up their minds.

As Stephen was about to get his chance to speak, apparently something really strange happened: everyone could see that his face looked like the face of an angel. I don't know exactly what that means; but that's what the witnesses who were there keep saying about it.

Anyway, he began to speak, and I've heard that it was like he was giving them a lesson about their own history! He reminded them how important Abraham was and about the promises that Yahweh made to him about a new land. He mentioned Joseph and told some of the story of what happened back in Egypt. He reminded them of how God kept his promises. Then he mentioned Moses. I guess he had to, given that they were accusing him of speaking against Moses! And he said that Moses did exactly what God asked of him and even though the people of Israel took a bit of convincing, God still kept his promises—which was the reason that they eventually entered into the land that Abraham was first told about. It was there that eventually King Solomon built the temple—the temple that they were accusing him of speaking against.

Now, I think the temple is a beautiful building. But—and don't get me wrong, I know it's an important place—it seems to me that God, the Father of Jesus who I've been hearing so much about, is more concerned with the people in and around the temple than he is with the actual temple itself.

And Stephen, too, seemed to be saying that those bigwigs had lost sight of what was really important. They were more concerned with buildings or laws, and not very concerned with what Yahweh had done for them or what Yahweh asked of them.

So he told them off!

He called them "stiff-necked people" with uncircumcised hearts and ears! He said things like "You are just like your fathers: you always resist the Holy Spirit!" He accused their ancestors of persecuting prophets, killing even those who predicted the coming of the Righteous One. And then he said, "And now you have betrayed and murdered him". He accused them of receiving the law that was given by angels but not obeying it.

That didn't go down too well with these powerful men who pride themselves on knowing the law and appearing to obey it!

They were furious. They gnashed their teeth at him.

But Stephen just … well … *glowed* is one description I've heard. He turned his face up towards heaven, and with a face full of the most profound peace said, "Look, I see heaven open and the Son of Man standing at the right hand of God".

They didn't want to hear. They covered their eyes, and they screamed at him, and dragged him out of the council to a place outside the city. We followed, hoping against hope that they would relent and understand what he was trying to tell them about Jesus. They threw him to the dusty ground and picked up rocks. We looked around, again hoping that someone would intervene, that they would stop.

But they didn't stop. They began to stone him. Witnesses and officials stood around watching, approving. No-one came to his aid.

It was awful to watch, but there was not a single thing that we could do.

And then Stephen prayed, "Lord Jesus, receive my spirit"; and as he fell to his knees, astonishingly, he cried out "Lord, do not hold this sin against them". And he died.

It was awful; but it was also extraordinary.

Bible study

Reflection/discussion point

"In Western Christianity, believers seem more concerned with fulfilment than with sacrifice." Do you agree or disagree with this statement? Why?

Pray that this study would help you to hear the word of God and respond to it in a way that is pleasing to him.

Read John 15:18-16:4a

1. Considering the whole passage, why did the world hate Jesus?

2. What is it about Jesus that made the people of the world guilty of sin?

3. Is it unexpected that the world would hate Jesus? Why?

4. If the world hates Jesus, what was so special about Jesus choosing his disciples from the world?

5. Given that the world has such a problem with Jesus, what will that mean for his disciples?

6. What or who will Jesus give to comfort and support his disciples?

7. What is the picture that Jesus paints for the time ahead when he is no longer present with his disciples? Why tell them about this?

8. What does Jesus ask of his disciples (despite the fact that they will face opposition)?

Implications

- Fast forward through the cross and the resurrection to our present reality. Does this teaching apply for believers today? Why or why not?

- Jesus seems more concerned to set a realistic expectation than to promise a comfortable existence for believers. How, if in any way, is this helpful for a believer?

- What are the dangers for a Christian in ignoring or avoiding the kind of suffering that Jesus talks about in this passage?

- Make a list of some of the good things that a believer is given now that will help to encourage resilience in suffering (e.g. other believers, forgiveness of sin, a church family, the Bible, hope).

Ready for the challenge

> The ultimate measure of a man is not where he stands in moments of comfort and convenience, but where he stands at times of challenge and controversy.

So said Martin Luther King Jr, the great American civil rights leader and preacher—first in a sermon, and then, in slightly modified form, in an address that he delivered at a Nobel Peace Prize Recognition Dinner on 27 January 1965.[7]

It is a profound statement and one that many Christians should be able to relate to. Christians can *say* what they believe, but that belief is most clearly tested, and most obvious, when Christians have to *stand firm* through challenge, conflict or persecution.

Suffering may not be a particularly popular notion, or even a feature that Christians would want to add into a list

---

7   ML King Jr, *A Gift of Love: Sermons from strength to love and other preachings*, Beacon Press, 1965, p 27. The Nobel Peace Prize Recognition Dinner address was titled 'The Struggle for Racial Justice' and is published in C Carson (ed), *The Autobiography of Martin Luther King Jr*, Grand Central Publishing, 2001.

of essential elements of being a person of faith. That said, according to the Bible and according to historical experience, the plain fact is that Christians suffer (individually and collectively) for their faith in Jesus. Rather than dismiss or ignore the notion, this chapter aims to acknowledge suffering so that when it is experienced, the Christian (together with the Christian family) will be ready to stand firm, resilient in that moment of challenge or controversy.

There are many passages in the New Testament that speak of pressure or persecution that come because of faith.[8] I have chosen to focus mostly on the letter of 1 Peter as it effectively asks the question, "If you are going to live for Christ, are you willing to make a stand?" It is a 'rubber-hits-the-road' kind of letter.

A Christ-centred hope

In the first third of the letter, Peter speaks about a Christ-centred hope (1:3-2:10). He wants his readers to be grounded in what God has done to save them and make them his chosen ones. He says, "In his great mercy [God] has given us new birth into a living hope through the resurrection of Jesus Christ from the dead" (1:3). This is cause for celebration. The inheritance that is given cannot be taken away—it will "never perish, spoil or fade" (1:4). Yet with that hope will sit some hard things. He goes on to say, "In all this you greatly rejoice, though now for a little while you may have had to suffer grief in all kinds of trials" (1:6). For all

8   For example, John 15:18-16:15; Acts 9:16; Rom 5:1-5; 2 Cor 1:3-7, 4:8-12; Phil 1:12-30; 2 Thess 1:3-5; 2 Tim 2:8-10, 3:10-15; Heb 10:32-35.

the good, there will be some hard things that will be part of your experience in faith. And there is a reason. These griefs come so that your faith will be proved genuine and result in the praise, glory and honour being rightly given when Jesus returns (1:7). Peter then finishes the section by describing the outcome of that Christ-centred hope: "You are a chosen people, a royal priesthood, a holy nation, God's special possession, that you may declare the praises of him who called you out of darkness into his wonderful light" (2:9).

Before we consider anything of the trials that suffering may cause, it is important to remember that every Christian has a living hope, as a chosen one, for an eternal birth—that is a hope that even suffering or death cannot take away.

Living with a Christ-centred hope

Peter continues, and in the middle section of the letter he helps his readers to understand how to live with a Christ-centred hope (2:11-4:11). He says, "Live such good lives among the pagans that, though they accuse you of doing wrong, they may see your good deeds and glorify God on the day he visits us" (2:12).

Peter recognizes the reality that Christians are living in a world that is not particularly favourable towards believers. Christians live under the rule of non-believing authorities, they work for non-believing masters (bosses), some are married to non-believing spouses, and they are called to live under the watchful eye of non-believing communities who will often mock, ridicule and, in many places around the world, hurt or kill them. His point: living like Christ should look very different to living for the world.

Suffering under a Christ-centred hope

In the final section of his letter, Peter wants to ensure that his readers understand what it means to suffer under a Christ-centred hope (4:12-5:11). This letter is especially helpful in the way it speaks to a body of believers (the church, collectively) and yet has so much to say that may be helpful for the individual Christian.

The opening part of this section of the letter is helpful in considering what it means to be resilient when suffering:

> [12] Dear friends, do not be surprised at the fiery ordeal that has come on you to test you, as though something strange were happening to you. [13] But rejoice inasmuch as you participate in the sufferings of Christ, so that you may be overjoyed when his glory is revealed. [14] If you are insulted because of the name of Christ, you are blessed, for the Spirit of glory and of God rests on you. [15] If you suffer, it should not be as a murderer or thief or any other kind of criminal, or even as a meddler. [16] However, if you suffer as a Christian, do not be ashamed, but praise God that you bear that name. [17] For it is time for judgement to begin with God's household; and if it begins with us, what will the outcome be for those who do not obey the gospel of God? [18] And,
>
>> "If it is hard for the righteous to be saved,
>> what will become of the ungodly and the sinner?"
>
> [19] So then, those who suffer according to God's will should commit themselves to their faithful Creator and continue to do good. (1 Pet 4:12-19)

Suffering is mentioned six times in these few verses, and as you look at those verses more closely, you'll notice that Peter is not referring to *general* suffering—the verses are not about sickness, poverty or injury; they are not about the pressures of school or college or university or work deadlines; and they are not about the grief that is felt when a loved one is dying.

The suffering that Peter addresses is the kind of suffering a believer endures when standing firm in faith.

Living for Christ

To prepare his readers for the hard truth about suffering, Peter describes some *trials* and then offers some *benefits*. He says, "Do not be surprised at the fiery ordeal that has come on you to test you, as though something strange were happening to you" (v 12).

This is about expectations. If you are not mentally prepared for tough stuff, how will you cope when that hard stuff hits? We are far more likely to succeed at something hard if we recognize up-front that it won't be easy.

If Jesus suffered at the hands of those he came to save, then his followers shouldn't be surprised that the same thing might happen to them (cf. John 15:18, as we saw in the Bible study above). As you live as a Christian, and as you talk about your faith, you presumably do so in order that others might be saved—so don't be surprised if this is a painful exercise. "Fiery ordeal" is sometimes translated "painful trial". The whole language of "ordeal" and "trial" and "test" should help Christians see that there is a purpose. It is a process that tests and strengthens us. It is to prepare us. It is to help us to be able to persevere when things get harder.

Bear in mind that the ordeal or trial that will be the cause of suffering will look different for every Christian. Generally, for Western Christians in parts of the world where Christianity is tolerated, suffering may involve pressures that

Christians experience for standing firm in their faith—perhaps false accusations, ridicule, job losses, career limitation, diminished reputation or social isolation. This appears to be an ever-increasing reality. For those Christians living in parts of the world where being a Christian is not tolerated or is illegal, Christians will often endure threats, restrictions, violence, persecution and injury (even to the point of death) against themselves and their loved ones. Suffering for faith takes many forms.

Next, Peter says something surprising: "Rejoice inasmuch as you participate in the sufferings of Christ, so that you may be overjoyed when his glory is revealed" (v 13).

If I were listening to the world, I would think that this was a typo. Rejoice that you participate in the sufferings of Christ? That is such a countercultural idea.

How is it possible to find anything good in something that is always hard? You may think you can't; but that is the lie our world tells. It is possible that in suffering there is joy.

Don't confuse what it means to be "overjoyed" with the secular view of happiness. Here, 'joy' and 'happiness' are not the same thing. When anyone suffers there is little reason to be happy about it. Calling upon someone to 'just be happy' ignores the reality of a hard situation. And bear in mind that when we experience something *hard*, that does not necessarily mean it is *bad*. To rejoice in suffering, however, looks beyond the immediate circumstance and comforts the Christian by pointing them to the future—a glorious future.

Look at the cross: great, unimaginable suffering; but suffering that delivers great, unending joy. Suffering for the Christian is not a threat, it is a promise—but with that promise comes the reality that your suffering in Christ shows that you belong to him. Believers who suffer for Christ have hope. That hope will be realized when his glory is revealed, and then you will be overjoyed.

Strategies

With those trials in mind, Peter offers three quick strategies.

First, remember that **you have some powerful help on your side**. "If you are insulted because of the name of Christ, you are blessed, for the Spirit of glory and of God rests on you" (v 14).

I remember a time when I found myself in a playground argument and I was at the mercy of some bullies a couple of years my senior. Being pushed around and insulted was not particularly comfortable. It was short-lived, though, because my older cousin seated nearby saw what was going on and very quickly came to my defence. All of a sudden, my fear of these bullies changed to great joy as they found themselves at the mercy of my older cousin. It is helpful when you have someone powerful on your side!

Having the name of Christ will attract insult. But the benefit is that you have a powerful ally. In your corner is "the Spirit of glory and of God".

Second, recognize that **you are not suffering because you deserve it**. "If you suffer, it should not be as a murderer or thief or any other kind of criminal, or even as a meddler" (v 15).

If you are reading this book, it is likely that you have fairly open access to Christian resources, unlike many of our brothers and sisters who live in countries where it is against the law to be Christian. Their experience of suffering for their faith is far deeper; it is desperate and devastating, and greater by an order of magnitude than many Western Christians could even comprehend.

If you "suffer" for your faith, it is not because you are getting your just desserts. God is not pointing the finger at you and accusing you of being in the wrong. This truth applies to all Christians—be they under the threat of the state, at the mercy of extremism, faced with family ostracization, or at risk of professional disadvantage.

In God, who knows exactly what all people do and say, we have a Father who never makes wrong judgements—in fact, his judgements always put what is wrong right.

Third, realize that **you have no reason to be ashamed; instead, praise God.** "If you suffer as a Christian, do not be ashamed, but praise God that you bear that name" (v 16).

Some one hundred years after Christ walked on earth, the Christian church had been established and was growing so large that the empire of the day saw it as a threat to their rule. So the Romans started to kill Christians in order to stop the growth. The plan failed. Those who saw how willing the Christians were to stand for their belief in Jesus took notice.

One of the Christian leaders, a man called Ignatius (the bishop of Antioch, which is in modern day Syria), was so eager that God be glorified that he was willing to be thrown to the lions so that others would see his faith. He wrote a letter to the churches in Rome recognizing that it was likely that he would "be a meal for the beasts", that his body would be "ground fine by the lions' teeth", that they would not leave "the smallest scrape of flesh" behind. His comfort was that he was dying for God as Jesus Christ's disciple.[9]

9   Ignatius, 'The Epistles to the Romans', *Early Christian Writings*, Penguin, 1968, p 86.

What Ignatius experienced is very similar to what millions of Christians have experienced across the centuries to this very day. Under Satan, the aim of any faith-generated persecution against Christians will be to prevent people hearing about Jesus so that they won't come to believe in him. Ignatius' letter illustrates the way that he rejoiced in the suffering that he received for his faith. He was eager to live so that God would get the glory. If you suffer for being a Christian, don't be ashamed; instead, praise God.

Suffering and judgement

Personally, I don't really like the idea of suffering, even for a good cause.

I wonder what the original readers of 1 Peter might have been thinking as they contemplated all the different kinds of suffering that might lie before them. Like us, I am sure they would have been uncertain.

Peter seems to have understood that uncertainty, and offers some perspective by looking at the role judgement plays in suffering:

> For it is time for judgement to begin with God's household; and if it begins with us, what will the outcome be for those who do not obey the gospel of God? And,
>
> > "If it is hard for the righteous to be saved,
> > what will become of the ungodly and the sinner?"
> > (1 Pet 4:17-18)

There is a theological truth exposed here—judgement involves everyone. It starts with the family of God, so it starts with Christians, and then it continues until all are judged.

The purpose of judgement is not only to point out what

is bad and wrong; it is also to point out what is good and right. If someone wrongs you, the judgement *against* them is also a judgement *for* you. It shows them to be in error and it shows you to be right.

The good news for those who have heard and accepted the gospel is that although Christians experience the judgement of God, so do those who oppose God. If it is tough for the righteous, then it will be even tougher for the ungodly.

Unbelievers don't suffer for faith in Jesus (because they don't *have* faith in Jesus), but what Peter points out is that they will still be judged, and without Jesus, they will not be saved.

That means that for persecuted Christians, judgement will put things right and the wrong that has been directed towards them will be dealt with eventually. God's judgement will leave those who have persecuted the family of God with little to stand upon.

Let us dig a little deeper.

Peter quotes Proverbs 11:31, which reads "If the righteous *receive their due on earth*, how much more the ungodly and the sinner!" Going back to the original quote helps us to see the intent behind what Peter is trying to teach. This does not mean that the salvation of believers is in any doubt. In an eternal sense, "the righteous" are saved by Jesus from the consequences of sin. What it does mean, however, is that those who are trying to live righteously in this fallen world will still sometimes find it hard to live out their salvation ("If it is hard for the righteous to be saved ..."; v 18). The experience of suffering on earth, although sometimes tough, is part of the judgement of God. In other words, the consequences of judgement are felt to some degree while Christians still live on earth.

That may very well mean that the suffering that Christians experience on earth (even at the hands of others) is part of the judgement of God. But that experience of judgement is limited to what is experienced on earth. It is a different story for those who have rejected God—they experience the consequence of God's judgement both now *and* later!

The apostle Paul in Romans 1 describes the judgement of God against "all the godlessness and wickedness of people who suppress the truth by their wickedness" (v 18). God's judgement was experienced in Paul's present day as "God gave them over in the sinful desires of their hearts" (v 24), as "God gave them over to shameful lusts" (v 26), and as "God gave them over to a depraved mind, so that they [did] what ought not to be done" (v 28). The consequence of sin— of rebellion—is experienced not just at the end of time, but in the present time.

Consider what that means for the righteous ones who live in this same world: while judgement is being experienced in the world, there will be suffering.

Christ-shaped suffering

In the garden of Gethsemane, shortly before he was arrested and knowing that he would die, Jesus prayed: "My Father, if it is not possible for this cup to be taken away unless I drink it, may your will be done" (Matt 26:42).

Jesus didn't like suffering either! To pray that the "cup" (the suffering) might be taken away, and if not, that God's will might be done regardless, is a prayer that shows us his dread of the suffering that he knew was ahead of him, but also demonstrates the trust that Jesus the Son had in God his Father.

Peter finishes this section of the letter encouraging

believers to have the same attitude as Christ Jesus: "So then, those who suffer according to God's will should commit themselves to their faithful Creator and continue to do good" (1 Pet 4:19; cf. 4:1).

When Christians suffer with the same attitude as Christ, they do that according to God's will. They "commit themselves to their faithful Creator", and while they wait they continue to do the good that he calls them to do.

Living now

So how does a Christian become more resilient in suffering? Here are some practical suggestions:

1. Pray

It is a brave person who prays that they may suffer for the sake of Christ! Prayer is one thing that you can do under any circumstance of suffering. And listening to your prayers is our Father in heaven. You could pray that suffering might stop (although the Bible doesn't promise it will). You could pray that you will be rescued (although God may have plans for you in your suffering). Don't pray that those who make you suffer will be punished (that is not how Jesus prayed). Instead, pray that you would be strengthened and obedient through your suffering.

2. Reset your expectations

Peter's suggestion is to have the same attitude as Christ. Expect that a part of the Christian life (but not all of it) will involve some tough stuff, and that this will be most acute when you stand for your faith. Peter's strategy in the face of

the suffering was to *remember* the Lord, *recognize* that standing for Jesus does not put you at fault, and *realize* that there
is no reason to be ashamed (1 Pet 4:14-16).

3. Remember your Christian family

You have been given a Christian family who can be a wonderful support to you, and whom you are also called to
support. When suffering, your Christian family can help to
recharge you (under God) so that you can continue to stand
firm for Jesus (see Heb 10:24-25). Recognize further that if
every Christian suffers for their faith, then you also have
a role in supporting other brothers and sisters in Christ,
whether they are the people whom you see regularly or the
ones who are scattered around the world proclaiming Christ
in locations that may be far more dangerous than your own.
Pray for other Christians who experience different degrees
of suffering or persecution from yours (see Eph 6:18-20). Pray
that God would provide for their needs, protect them from
harm, help them to persevere in faith, and enable them to
continue to proclaim Christ despite opposition.

4. Proclaim Jesus

Know what you believe so that when put on the spot, you
are able to stand firm for Jesus (see Eph 6:14-17, 19-20). One
of the best ways to defend yourself is to continue to proclaim Christ (see John 15:27).

5. Love those who make you suffer

In the "Sermon on the Mount", Jesus taught his disciples
to "love your enemies and pray for those who persecute
you" (Matt 5:44; cf. Rom 12:14, 17-21). There is a humility

that demonstrates a Christlike attitude which is on display whenever a Christian suffers.

• • •

Christian suffering, when put into a Christ-shaped perspective, calls for a resilience that trusts that God will one day put all things right. Christians should live out the good will of God not just in times of comfort and convenience, but also in times of challenge, conflict or persecution ...

> And the God of all grace, who called you to his eternal glory in Christ, *after you have suffered a little while*, will himself restore you and make you strong, firm and steadfast. To him be the power for ever and ever. Amen. (1 Pet 5:10)

What's best next?

- What aspects of your thinking and your behaviour should be changed as a result of reflecting on this 'essential' Christian quality?

- What step can you take this week to make that change?

Pray about it.

6. COMMITTED IN MEMBERSHIP

The world says: Put yourself first, and put
others next—if it's convenient.

But God says: Love me above all else, and love
others before yourself.

A voice from Acts: "United around Jesus."

Inspired by Acts 15:1-21

We've been dealing with quite a delicate problem!

It's been a difficult time for our church—but thankfully, with God's help, we have found a way through it and our church family is not divided. It was a close-run thing, though …

Let me explain.

At first, it was simply an exciting time for us, being a new church. People from all kinds of backgrounds were coming to hear about Jesus, and as we talked about him they put their trust in him. The kingdom of God was growing, and we were right there in the middle of it!

Even better: many of those who became part of the church were Jewish people from Jerusalem and all around Judea. All their lives they had been reading in their old Scriptures about a Messiah, and now for the first time, they had come to realise that this Messiah was, in fact, Jesus! It was wonderful when they became brothers and sisters in faith.

I was born a Jew, and as our church life together began I loved the fact that we had a rich heritage. We're descendants of Israel, and with that we brought a deep understanding of the Scriptures, and traditions that had been part of our culture for centuries.

But people from other areas, too, were also hearing about Jesus and believing—places like Samaria and Phoenicia; regions where far more people were Gentile and where our history and traditions were not known. This was exciting too! We were so thankful for Paul and Barnabas, who had gone travelling to share the good news with both Jews and Gentiles across Asia Minor.

Followers of Jesus everywhere welcomed people from far and wide with open arms, overjoyed to hear how God had been working in their lives. The church grew everywhere, not only in number but in diversity—and in complexity.

I guess we should have predicted that when people of different cultural backgrounds came together there would be things to sort out! After all, Jews and Gentiles had not always got on. The process of becoming one family was always going to have some hiccups.

The issue was about circumcision. You see, according to what Moses taught the Israelites, those who were the people of God were to be marked by the sign of circumcision. This was an important part of how they were to stand out, as God's people, from all the other nations.

Now, although I had become Christian, I was obviously still circumcised—and that remains an important part of who I am (couldn't really change it!). But some people like me, with a Jewish background, had begun telling people that unless they were circumcised, they couldn't be saved. And that was causing problems for the Gentiles who were converting and becoming part of our church—they thought they were becoming Christian, not Jewish!

So Paul and Barnabas returned to Jerusalem, and we held a church family meeting—a council—to discuss the issue. It was great when Paul and Barnabas arrived. All the apostles and elders were there and the whole church welcomed them back, eager to hear about all the people who had joined the Christian family.

But then it was down to business. Some of our number who had been Pharisees and knew the law well suggested that for the Gentiles to be accepted into the church family, they had to be circumcised and were required to obey the law of Moses. There was much discussion about this, but no agreement was reached.

Eventually, Peter got up to try and settle the dispute. And what he had to say really mattered, because very early on, back when he was staying with Cornelius in Caesarea, the Lord had made it clear to Peter that God showed no favouritism and wanted Gentiles also to hear the message of the gospel.

Peter told us all, "We believe it is through the grace of our Lord Jesus Christ that we are saved, just as the Gentiles are". He said that we shouldn't test God by putting obligations on disciples that just make it harder to live as Christians. Then Paul and Barnabas stood and spoke about some of the amazing things that God had done among the Gentiles.

And then it was my turn. As the brother of Jesus and also a leader in our church, I thought it was important that we stay united around Jesus and not the law. After all, our prophet Amos had long ago foretold that both Jews and Gentiles would bear the name of our Lord.

So I suggested that we remove circumcision as a requirement when turning to God (and I I'm sure the Gentile men have been relieved to hear that!). Although circumcision might be important for my fellow Jews, I could see that it was more important that our church family lived for Jesus—and circumcision had nothing to do with our salvation.

I wasn't throwing out the law, as some may have initially thought! The law is still helpful, particularly in highlighting areas of our lives that might be displeasing to the Lord. It was widely known that many Gentiles, prior to becoming Christian, had engaged in idolatry, sacrifices and sexual immorality; and so I suggested that we advise our new brothers and sisters to avoid those things. Any believer engaging in those practices, irrespective of whether they had a Jewish or a Gentile background, would be discrediting Jesus.

I am sure that, in years to come, believers all around the world will be challenged by lots of different things that will threaten to undermine their faith and discredit Jesus. That's why it's so important that we are all one *in him*. One of the wonderful things about being a church family is that we can help one another live well for Jesus.

The council where we thrashed out these matters was hard—conflict always is! But it turned out to be a great thing to do—because it drew us together around Jesus, and helped us to really care for others in Christ.

Bible study

Once upon a time, there was a tribe that lived in a hidden area of the Amazon jungle. They had a custom that brought all the family groups together for a feast once a year. Each family group would bring a container of drink (supposedly made from their harvested crops) as an offering to the 'fellowship'. Each container was poured into one large vat and stirred, creating an amazing mixture that symbolically demonstrated their unity as a collective tribe. And then, to celebrate, they poured a portion for each member and they all drank as one.

One year a miracle happened. When everyone took their drink, they realised it was quite simply ... plain water!

Why? Because each family group had brought only water, thinking that all the other family groups would cover for them. They all offered nothing, and as a result, their collective experience was a failure.

Reflection/discussion point

In what ways could you and your church relate to this made-up story?

Pray that this study would help you to hear the word of God and respond to it in a way that is pleasing to him.

Read 1 Corinthians 12:12-31

1. The apostle Paul paints a picture for the Corinthian church of what it should mean to be members of the "one body" (vv 12, 13) of Christ. Do you think he is talking about all Christians everywhere or only about the Corinthian church?

2. As you look across these verses, notice that the Father (God), the Spirit and the Son (Christ) are all mentioned. What role does each one play in bringing this body together?

3. Who is it that determines the "parts" of the body? What is not permissible for those parts? How is that expressed in a church?

4. Why does Paul make a distinction between parts that are unpresentable and those that are presentable? What is his point? What is his purpose?

5. In verses 27-31, the one body with its many parts is described and there are many different appointed parts. Is this meant to be an exhaustive list (cf. Rom 12:4-8; Eph 4:11-13)? What is the point of having people appointed to different roles in the church?

6. Go back and read what comes directly before this passage, in 1 Corinthians 12:4-11. What does it tell you about the nature of the "different kinds of gifts" (v 4)? And to what end should these various gifts be used?

7. 1 Corinthians 12 does not explicitly state this fact (as Colossians 1:18 does), but the context implicitly suggests it: Who is the head of this body? How is that significant?

Implications

- In what ways is this passage countercultural to the society we live in?

- What would be an 'un-body-like' response to this passage?

- In what ways does this passage favourably describe your church?

- Does this passage challenge you in your attitude/activity/ministry at church? How?

Suggestions for prayer
- Give thanks that in Christ you are part of a body that is both diverse and united.
- Pray for opportunities to play a committed part in the body for the common good.

Membership

'Membership' is a fairly common idea. We have memberships of libraries, sports clubs, magazines or journals, road service organizations, schools, clubs, gyms, churches and much more.

We become members to secure some benefit. It may be the ability to borrow books, or to secure good seats to watch the cricket or football, or to receive the magazines that interest us, or to have guaranteed assistance if the car breaks down. We may become members to help a school to give our children a better education, or to have a vote in the club that we belong to, or to gain cheaper entry to be able to use exercise equipment. You get the drift.

In many ways, the benefits of membership in our secular world mirror those of membership in a church, but not completely—there is a difference.

Secular membership is almost always entirely for personal benefit, and while there is personal benefit for those who are members of a church, that is not the driving motivation for church membership.

Church membership should be about loving and serving God, and his people, before ourselves.

What is church?

This essential Christian principle is about being committed in membership in a church community. Before thinking about what it means to be committed to a church, we need to understand what church is!

Very simply, church is an assembly of God's people.

It is a place where there is a distinction between God's chosen people and those who reject God.

The word for 'church' in our English Bibles is a translation of the Greek word *ekklesia*. It literally means to 'call (*kaleo*) out (*ek*)'. In other words, 'church' is a body of people who are 'called out' by God to join together as his people—the followers of his Son.

It is a family. It is a place where worship is exercised. It is a place where the people of God serve him and others before themselves.

If you have been a Christian for some length of time, then the church is your spiritual family—a place where those in Christ belong. And if you are new in your Christian walk, then the church is a gathering of adopted brothers and sisters whom God has given you to walk alongside you in faith.

While it should be a place where the stranger is welcomed and addressed, it should never be a place where the person of the world has greater influence than the person of God. When Christians gather, they gather in what should be a safe place and one where they are spurred on in their Christian life and witness. It should be inevitable that what a church family offers is distinctly different to what the world offers.

When you became a Christian, your membership in the church took both a *universal* and a *local* shape—a wide and a narrow view, if you like.

Universal church

The church *universal* is the worldwide body of believers who meet in various locations and times around the world, have met throughout history, and who all profess faith in Jesus as Lord.

Brothers and sisters around the world who are fleeing from persecution, those who are on the mission field, those who meet as Christians around your country, and those who meet in the churches in suburbs around your city— all of these are members with you of the universal church, because we all have the same Lord and Saviour in Jesus.

Jesus speaks of the universal church. When he said to

his disciple Peter in Matthew 16:18, "I will build my church", he probably did not have in mind a specific local church on the corner of King David Street and Goliath Avenue in Jerusalem! What he meant was that he would build together all those in the years to come who would be his followers, the members of his body—his universal church.

When the apostle Paul says he suffers "for the sake of [Christ's] body, which is the church" (Col 1:24), he is referring to the universal church—all those who are members in Christ. And he refers to the universal church when he writes to Timothy about "God's household, which is the church" (1 Tim 3:15).

Scripture testifies to the importance of being part of the universal church where we stand shoulder to shoulder with others in faith—even though we may not speak the same language, be from the same culture, have the same lifestyles, live in the same kinds of material circumstances, or even live in the same era of history.

Whenever I spend time with Christians of other cultures or languages, I recognize a beautiful reality—I have more in common with these brothers and sisters in faith than I do with many who don't yet know Jesus even though they live in my own suburb or city!

Local church

Scripture also testifies to the importance of the local church.

The church *local* is your immediate church fellowship— the group of Christians with whom you share life, face to face, week in and week out. These are the brothers and sisters who know you by name, who pray specifically for you, who help carry your burdens, who celebrate your successes and mourn your losses, and who help you to love and know God better and to serve him and others as you work to grow God's kingdom.

Paul addresses the local church in 1 and 2 Corinthians ("To the church of God in Corinth"), Ephesians ("To God's holy people in Ephesus"), 1 and 2 Thessalonians ("To the church of the Thessalonians") and Philippians ("To all God's holy people in Christ Jesus at Philippi"). In Colossians, he sends a greeting to "Nympha and the church in her house" (Col 4:15). There is a very particular local church that he has in mind.

As you meet each week with a body of believers, you express your membership in a local church.

Both ... and ...

As Christians, it is important to recognize that we belong to both the *universal* church and the *local* church. Why?

For one thing, quite obviously, there are many more Christians in the world than would be able to meet in your particular church space—but there is a time coming when all Christians will gather around the throne of Christ in eternity and worship as the full *universal* church. It is a wonderful blessing to recognize our place alongside so many others in Christ.

Yet it also matters that we meet together as a specific *local* church, on a regular basis, to serve God and others. Christians cannot gather as the universal church to hear the Bible taught and proclaimed, to baptize new believers, to sing songs of praise, to take the Lord's Supper together, to reach out to the communities around them, to serve one another, to hold one another accountable, to physically care for each other, or to urge one another on towards love and good deeds.

Meeting in local churches is important for the life and wellbeing of all Christians.

Draw near to God and to others

Hebrews is helpful. In chapter 10, the author writes to Christians who are losing confidence. Some are being persecuted, some are leaving the faith to avoid suffering, and others are abandoning Christ because they want to fit in with the world around them. His advice? Draw near to God and draw near to others:

> Since we have a great priest over the house of God, let us draw near to God with a sincere heart and with the full assurance that faith brings, having our hearts sprinkled to cleanse us from a guilty conscience and having our bodies washed with pure water. Let us hold unswervingly to the hope we profess, for he who promised is faithful. (Heb 10:21-23)

It is because of Jesus that the church even exists. He is the high priest who, by his blood, made it possible for sinners to be brought to God. The image here is of a washing—those who are sprinkled to be cleansed and washed with pure water are the ones able to draw near to God in full assurance of faith. They are Christians. They are the church. They are the ones who live by faith.

That is not all. Alongside faith, there is also hope. Hebrews calls Christians to draw near to God and to do that by holding unswervingly to the hope they have in Jesus. There is a straight road: don't veer to the left or the right; just look straight and go. By its very definition, hope stands before us, not behind—so press on in hope.

Christians should draw near to God in faith by pressing on with hope because of Jesus.

And there is more!

> And let us consider how we may spur one another on toward love and good deeds, not giving up meeting together, as some are in the habit of doing, but encouraging one another—and all the more as you see the Day approaching. (Heb 10:24-25)

Hebrews offers three tips here that help the Christian draw near to others.

1. Spur one another on

Any horse rider would know how to spur on a horse. Gently but firmly, you spur them to move by giving them a nudge in the ribs with your heels. The aim here is never to harm the horse, but to urge them forward for your mutual benefit. So it is in a church family. You never aim to cause harm, but you spur others on towards love and good deeds. The result should be mutually beneficial.

2. Meet together

It is very difficult to spur others on if you are not there! Evidently that was a problem for the recipients of this letter. Habitually, they *missed* opportunities to meet with one another. So the challenge is to instead make it a *habit to* meet together. I used to have a Bible study leader who would turn on his answering machine an hour before Bible study—and the message was "Let us not give up meeting together as some are in the habit of doing!"

3. Encourage one another

There is an end in view: it is the day that Jesus returns. It is a day when all that is wrong will be made right, all that is tiresome will be lifted away, and all that is perfect will be experienced fully—but that day is not here yet. As the tired athlete runs his race, so the Christian runs the race of faith. And as that athlete is buoyed when the crowd cheers for them, so is the Christian when their brothers and sisters encourage them along.

One of the benefits of being in a church family is that you can be a very real encouragement to others, and hopefully that is reciprocated.

• • •

In just a few verses, Hebrews has offered the Christian a way to persevere—and it is not alone.

At the time when this book was being written, many in the world were in lockdown due to the COVID-19 pandemic. To keep people safe, lockdown restrictions were issued that confined many to their homes, which meant that gathering physically was impossible. Thanks to many and various technologies, Christians found themselves "meeting together" online. COVID has helped to highlight the importance of continuing to meet together face to face, and how much better it is when that can happen physically. Yet even in the online world, what Hebrews teaches stands true—as Christians draw near to one another (in whatever gathering capacity) our intention should be to spur one another on, to regular-ly meet, and to encourage one another while we wait for Jesus to return. In doing so you draw near to God and draw near to others. That is a win-win!

Let's apply this to our church membership.

Universal church only: a vertical relationship

From time to time, I hear a believer say that they don't have to be a member of a particular local church, because they are 'in Christ'.

At a universal level, that is true. They can enjoy time with the Lord alone and pray quietly to him.

A few years ago, I was at a church and each Sunday a lady would join us. She would arrive in the middle of the first song, always sit in the same pew (off to the side), put her Bible on her lap and read or listen, and then, halfway through the final song, get up and leave. It took me a few months to get a conversation out of her. Her response: "I come here to worship God and him alone".

Now, I recognise that there are all sorts of reasons, traumas and anxieties that may lead a person to isolate themselves at church in this way.

That said, the risk of only focusing on the universal church is that you divorce yourself from serving the local church. The expression of your faith is only a *vertical* relationship. There is no accountability, no fellowship, no commitment to others. This can be seen as a rather self-centred expression of faith.

But, probably more alarmingly, it is also an attitude that rejects God's call both to gather and to love others.

Membership of God's universal church brings with it the requirement to be (as much as possible) a member of God's local church—to serve God *and* serve others. Christians do that by spurring others on, meeting together, and making it our job to encourage others.

That said, there are very valid reasons why people may not be able to make it each week to a local church—they could be sick (physically or mentally), in aged care, interstate, away with work, on holidays, on mission, or away on active service. And further, many people find it hard to be committed to a local church because of bad experiences—after all, when sinners gather (even forgiven sinners), we are far from perfect.

Be that as it may, no matter how hard, the church is worth fighting for and worth committing ourselves to, because it is created by and precious to God, and a wonderful and indispensable way in which he cares for and provides for his people in this world.

Avoid the trap of only attending church when there is nothing better on. Reject the idea of replacing church with one-off social, leisure or sporting activities (as important as your or your children's sporting ambitions may be). Don't be a believer who sits in the pews and offers your occasional attendance. Invest yourself in the life of your church family, because God has given you gifts and talents to use in some way (as we saw in 1 Corinthians 12 in the Bible study). If these gifts and talents are not used for serving among your Christian family, then we will be the weaker for it. For God's sake, for our sake, and for your own sake, consider how to be committed in membership.

Local church only: a horizontal relationship

Okay, we have looked at the danger of thinking that church is only a place where you do business with God—as if church membership is thinking only about the vertical relationship between you and God.

Let's consider the opposite danger.

There are times when a believer says that they are only committed to their local church. If Christians focus only on their local church then they run the risk of losing connection to the wider body and so becoming isolated and insular. The emphasis here is very *horizontal*.

Yes, there are times when the universal church, represented by Christians we don't even know, does things that are embarrassing, and it would be good to say it is just them and not us. Be that as it may, the Bible calls the church to do many things, some of which involve specialization (e.g. care for the widows, homeless, vulnerable, children, refugees)—and that is the church collective (or universal), not just the church individual (or local).

It is possible that God could have chosen to do all his work through each individual if he wanted to, but for some reason he has decided that it is best to give different gifts to different individuals who belong to different churches and then, through them, care for his world.

Drawing together individuals from a range of local churches gives them the opportunity to serve as part of the universal church in ways that make the most of their specific gifts and passions. Often this will lead to 'parachurch' organisations being formed ('para' is Greek for 'beside', so these are 'beside-church' organizations). In the country in which I live, there are terrific Christian organizations who do the specific work of reaching, training and caring for others.[10] All are examples of the universal church in action.

---

10 For some examples, consider: the Church Missionary Society, Bush Church Aid, City Bible Forum, Anglicare, BaptistCare, Compassion, Scripture Union, Baptist World Aid, Anglican Aid, Australian Fellowship of Evangelical Students, Ministry Training Strategy, Bible Society Australia, Living Faith, the Anglican Schools Corporation, Matthias Media (and other good theological publishing houses), and, of course, the denominations and theological colleges with which our local churches are affiliated. (This is not an exhaustive list.)

Our local church is made up of Christians who have often come to faith in Jesus through these Christian organizations. This is a two-way partnership; it cannot be one or the other. It is good for a Christian to find a way to be supportively involved at a universal level alongside their local involvement.

Committed in membership

Allow me to paint two contrasting pictures which will hopefully draw out the benefits of being committed in gospel membership.

Picture 1: the 'me-first' church

Imagine a church full of people who put the gospel second in their lives. A church with people who are there first and foremost for themselves. A church with people who do a lot of watching but are involved only a little. A place where people give lip service but not active service to the gospel. A place where people turn up when they don't have something else on that they prefer (sport, work, socializing, weekends away, etc.). A place that is more about social connection than a commitment to the gospel. A place where each person is more of a passenger than a driver—expecting a service. A place where helpful (and sometimes hard) things can't be said to spur one another on. A place where accountability is only an ideal.

This is a confusing place, because it's not clear what it means to be Christian—as being Christian is not obvious in the deeds of its 'members'. It's a place where many people have acquaintances only, because they aren't there regularly enough to make friends.

The 'me-first' church is not the church that the New Testament paints as the model church.

Picture 2: the 'love-God-then-others' church

Now imagine a church full of people who put the gospel first. A church where members ask, "What does the gospel ask of me?" A church where people grasp hold of each other in responsibility and love. A church where repentance is valued, belief is honoured, and obedience encouraged. A church that reflects a confidence in the blood of Jesus. A church where, each week, what is taught and sung and read and prayed is intentional and taken seriously. A church where people serve for the sake of others and even at their own expense.

This is a place where someone can be taught, rebuked, corrected and encouraged without offence or indignation. It's a place where there can be loving accountability. A place where people can spur others on towards love and good deeds. A place where people protect their time to ensure that they meet together. A place where there is ownership and intentionality. It's a place where friendships really matter.

The 'love-God-then-others' church is the church that the New Testament paints as the model church. It is also the church that sounds far more attractive and worthwhile.

Being committed in gospel membership is about loving God and loving others before ourselves. Being committed in gospel membership is about putting the gospel first.

Getting practical with membership

Here are ten practical suggestions which may seem obvious, yet may help you to express your membership in church.

- During the week leading up to church, **read the Bible passage** that will be preached on. Remember to take your Bible with you to church.[11]
- **Plan to be there, and plan to be there before the start time!** If it takes you 15 minutes to travel to church, then give yourself 25 minutes.
- If you drive, **park furthest away**—not miles away, but far enough so that you will allow others to have more convenient parking spots.
- If it is the custom of your church, **wear a name tag/label** (yes, I know it can be dorky, but it sure helps people relate to each other more easily—and newcomers are served).
- When you arrive, **look for someone you don't know** and, paying no attention to appearance, culture, age or gender, sit with them.
- **Avoid sitting at the end** of a seat row or pew as it blocks off the rest of the row.
- **Pray**—for the church, for the people who will sit nearby, for the preacher, for what will be preached, and for opportunities to talk about Jesus.

---

11 Like many people, you may be in the habit of using a Bible app on your phone. In this digital age we do so much on our phones, including reading our Bibles, and it's very convenient. But here's something I invite you to consider: I really like it when at church people look at their hard-copy Bibles, (a) because I know that they are looking at the Bible and not at social media or something else; and (b) because it clearly says to all around (including any newcomers) that looking at the Bible is important (otherwise it may look like people are uninterested and simply scrolling on their phones when the Bible is being taught!).

- **Fill in a comment card or welcome card** (even if you are a core member of the church)—if others see you doing this, it will help those who are new or unsure to feel better about giving their details.
- **Sing** with joy, **listen** with interest, **think** with discernment, **speak** with grace.
- **Plan to stay and chat after the gathering**—or kick on for lunch or dinner—and use the opportunity to talk at some point about what you heard at church.

• • •

Christians should find a *local church* and be committed to that body of believers—with their time, energy, money, service, presence and skill. And Christians should find a *universal church* ministry and be committed to it—in prayer, service, support, money, involvement and concern.

What's best next?

- What aspects of your thinking and your behaviour should be changed as a result of reflecting on this 'essential' Christian quality?

- What step can you take this week to make that change?

Pray about it.

7. LOVING IN RELATIONSHIPS

The world says: All you need is love—and we can define 'love' to be whatever we choose.

But God says: Love others in a way that is both pleasing and acceptable to me.

A voice from Acts: "I needed to obey ... even if it meant loving my enemy."

Inspired by Acts 9:10-19

Have you ever been asked to do something that just feels wrong?

I remember hearing God's call. And I remember thinking that *nothing* seemed right about what I was being asked to do!

As a follower of Jesus, I had been so encouraged to see the gospel work in Damascus going from strength to strength. More and more people in my home city were hearing about Jesus and becoming his disciples. It was exciting.

But then we heard a rumour. Saul of Tarsus was on his

way to Damascus. This was unsettling to say the least.

Saul had led the charge against many followers of 'the Way'. He had issued murderous threats against the Lord's disciples and had arranged permission from the high priest to travel around the synagogues seeking out Christians to imprison for their faith. He was a piece of work. There were even stories about him looking on approvingly as Stephen was stoned outside Jerusalem.

We all knew the threat he posed.

And then the Lord called out to me in a vision: "Ananias! Go to the house of Judas on Straight Street and ask for a man from Tarsus named Saul. He will be praying, and he will be expecting you, because in a vision he has seen a man named Ananias restore his sight."

What? Surely this was a cruel joke.

If this was the same man we feared, this was a suicide mission! I had to say something. "Lord," I said, "I have heard many reports about this man and all the harm that he has done to your holy people in Jerusalem. He has come here with authority from the chief priests to arrest all who call on your name!"

And I will never forget what the Lord said next. "Go! This man is my chosen instrument to proclaim my name to the Gentiles and their kings and to the people of Israel."

Now I had a choice. I could listen to my fear, reject the words I had heard from my Lord as a falsehood, and self-ishly walk the other way; or I could love like my Lord, which would require me to regard his words as truth and obey them—even if it meant loving my enemy.

I went to Straight Street.

Pushed open the door.

Cautiously entered the house.

Saw a man at prayer.

Looked at this man, who couldn't see me and didn't know I was there.

I still could have run. I wanted to. I *hated* the things that he had done.

But I placed my hands on him and said, "Brother Saul, the Lord—Jesus, who appeared to you on the road as you were coming here—has sent me so that you may see again and be filled with the Holy Spirit".

Immediately, a substance like scales fell from Saul's eyes. He could see again. It was all as the Lord had said it would be.

I am glad I didn't run. Saul was baptized, and ever since that moment he has served the Lord with more zeal than anyone I've known. Now he is known as Paul, the apostle to the Gentiles. What an unfathomable change!

It wasn't comfortable for me to do as God told me. This man was an enemy of *everything* I believed in. I did not want to love him—it all felt completely wrong! Yet now Paul is my brother in Christ. I am so glad that I trusted God and obeyed his call.

Bible study

Reflection/discussion point

Love is such an important concept. It is written about in books, sung about in songs, displayed in movies, and valued in relationships. Around our world and throughout the pages of the Bible, a lot of emphasis is placed on the desire to love and be loved. Is love something best understood as something that you *feel* or something that you *do*? Why?

Pray that this study would help you to hear the word of God and respond to it in a way that is pleasing to him.

Read Matthew 22:34-40

Matthew and Mark both record this interaction in their Gospels (cf. Mark 12:28-31). The Pharisees (the religious leaders of the day) tried to catch Jesus out by asking him about Old Testament law.

1. Why are laws (today) created?

2. In the Old Testament, in addition to the Ten Commandments, it has been suggested that there are around 613 laws and regulations. What is strange about asking Jesus which is the "greatest" (v 36) of those laws?

3. Does Jesus answer the question? How is the law applied in the way Jesus has answered?

   Note: It would be likely that the person listening to Jesus' answer would have expected him to quote one of the Ten Commandments (Exod 20:1-17; Deut 5:1-22). Instead, Jesus refers to Deuteronomy 6:5 ("Love the Lord your God with all your heart and with all your soul and with all your strength") and Leviticus 19:18 ("Love your neighbour as yourself").

4. When someone obeys a law, who benefits? When someone loves as Jesus suggests here, who benefits?

5. Is there anything offensive, alienating or objectionable in what Jesus is calling people to do?

6. Why do you think Jesus says, "All the Law and the Prophets hang on these two commandments" (v 40)? Is it that these two commandments make the rest redundant?

Read Romans 13:9-11

7. Here the apostle Paul refers to the commandments. What does he say fulfils the law?

8. Who is he calling upon to exercise this love? Why?

Implications

* In what ways is the instruction to love God wholeheartedly and to love others countercultural to the society we live in? Does doing one rather than the other diminish them both?

* How should a Christian apply this commandment to those we find hardest to love? Or to those who show no love in return? Or to those who might respond with hatred?

- Are there boundaries or limits to love? When a Christian exercises love, must it always be in a way that the other finds 'loving'?

- In what practical ways should obedience to Jesus' words be lived out by Christians today?

Suggestion for prayer

Create a list of ways in which you could show love both to God and to others. Then check what you have listed. Will any of your efforts be experienced by those who don't yet know the gospel? Pray about how you can show this love.

Perfect love

Love is a many-splendoured thing ... love is a battlefield ... love you to the moon ... you can't hurry love ... stupid love ... love hurts ... crazy little thing called love ... love is just a game ... love wins ... can't help falling in love ... all you need is love!

We only have to run through the titles of a few famous love songs to see our popular culture's take on how confusing the concept of love can be, and to see how it captures many different ideas that exist about that little word.

In modern society, 'love' is obviously highly valued—yet what it *means* to love seems like a very complicated question.

Essential to the Christian life is the call to be *loving*. 'Love' can be a very general term, so in this chapter, it is important to understand that we are considering *Christian love*—that is, a love for others that is both pleasing and acceptable to God.

And to do that, we turn to the letter of 1 John.[12] Like a layered wedding cake, 1 John raises several themes and stacks them upon one another. As we read, we make our way from layer to layer and see more of how the whole cake fits together. Helpfully, John shows us that if we misunderstand love (and let's face it, we all have at one time or another), then we find ourselves in all sorts of difficulties—regardless of whether we call ourselves Christians or not.

Let us start with the ideal—perfect love:

> Dear friends, let us love one another, for love comes from God. Everyone who loves has been born of God and knows God. Whoever does not love does not know God, because God is love. (1 John 4:7-8; cf. 4:16b)

John offers the template for perfect love by pointing to its origin: God himself. He is the backstory, the foundation, the

---

12 While I am primarily using 1 John in this chapter, godly love is a key theme that runs through both the Old and New Testaments. It's a big topic. Many of the Old Testament passages focus on the source of love (being God) while the New Testament passages are largely instructive as to how to love (in a godly way). See, for example, Exod 34:6-7; Deut 6:5; Pss 51:1-2, 86:5, 100:1-5, 146:6-9; Prov 3:3-4, 10:12, 17:17; Isa 54:10; Matt 5:43-48; John 15:9-17; Rom 12:9-21; 1 Corinthians 13, 16:14; Eph 4:1-2, 5:2; Col 3:12-14; 1 Pet 4:8.

reason why we have love at all. John says that whatever love is, it *starts* with God, it is best *expressed* in God, it is *exercised* thanks to God, it is *determined* most clearly by God, and it is *experienced* most effectively by anyone loving like God.

When we say 'God' here, we have in view the perfect relationship of the 'Godhead': God the Father, God the Son and God the Spirit. And John describes this trinitarian way of understanding what it means to live and experience God's love:

> This is how *God* showed his love among us: He sent his one and only son into the world that we might live through him. This is love: not that we loved God, but that he loved us and sent his Son as an atoning sacrifice for our sins. Dear friends, since God so loved us, we also ought to love one another. No-one has ever seen God; but if we love one another, God lives in us and his love is made complete in us.
>
> This is how we know that we live in him and he in us: He has given us of his *Spirit*. And we have seen and testify that the *Father* has sent his *Son* to be the Saviour of the world. If anyone acknowledges that Jesus is the Son of God, God lives in them and they in God. And so we know and rely on the love God has for us.
>
> God is love. *Whoever lives in love lives in God, and God in them.* (1 John 4:9-16)

To know the love of God, you have been given his Spirit, and the Spirit has been given in the context of what the Father did when he sent his Son to save you. Anyone who acknowledges Jesus as the Son lives in the love of God. To understand the nature of love, we look first at the relationship between the Father, Son and Spirit and how they, together, love us.

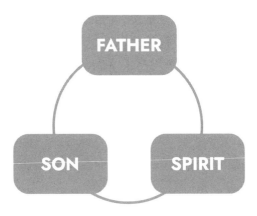

In the Godhead we see *perfect love*, *perfect truth* and *perfect obedience*. They are the perfect example of what loving one another should look like.

An implication, then, is that if you take God out of the picture, what you have is a tainted love. I do not mean to say that a person without God is incapable of love. Looking around our world we see countless examples of people from all walks of life experiencing and showing love—meaningful, real, genuine love.

Nevertheless, the kind of love that John has in mind is a *Christian love*, one that originates with God and is first demonstrated in the Godhead. In fact, it is that love that in turn gives Christians the template for how they should love: "since God so loved us, we also ought to love one another" (v 11). And that kind of love will be (by very nature) Christian, whether or not it is accepted by the world. *Christian love is a sacrificial love for others that is both pleasing and acceptable to God before it is to the world.*

Love, truth and obedience

Next, to understand love, it will help to understand how it is integrally connected to *truth* and to *obedience*, such that you cannot separate the three. These three ideas intersect with one another at almost every point. Without *love*, truth will not be valued. Without *truth*, it is difficult to know how to obey. Without *obedience*, it is impossible to demonstrate true love.

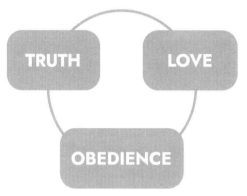

It would be helpful if John worked through each of those ideas one at a time. That is not his style; but we will look at each in turn.

Love

> [11] For this is the message you heard from the beginning: We should love one another. [12] Do not be like Cain, who belonged to the evil one and murdered his brother. And why did he murder him? Because his own actions were evil and his brother's were righteous. [13] Do not be surprised, my brothers and sisters, if the world hates you. [14] We know that we have passed from death to life, because we love each other.

¹⁵ Anyone who does not love remains in death. Anyone who hates a brother or sister is a murderer, and you know that no murderer has eternal life residing in him.

¹⁶ This is how we know what love is: Jesus Christ laid down his life for us. And we ought to lay down our lives for our brothers and sisters. (1 John 3:11-16)

Some context and then background will be helpful.

Just before this passage, John describes the difference between being a child of God and being a child of the devil (1 John 3:10). If you want to know whether you are a child of God, says John, presumably remembering what Jesus had taught him (cf. John 15:16-17), you should "love one another" (v 11). Then, to make the point, he tells the story of two family groups in the passage above. The first is the story of Cain ("Do not be like Cain ..."; v 12). The second is the story of Jesus ("Jesus Christ laid down his life ..."; v 16). Don't be like Cain. Be like Jesus.

Cain murdered his brother Abel as recorded back in Genesis 4. He was motivated by hate and envy. Both brothers presented offerings to the Lord. Cain presented some of the "fruits of the soil" and Abel gave "fat portions from some of the firstborn of his flock" (Gen 4:3-4). For an unstated reason, God looked in favour on Abel, not Cain (Gen 4:4-5). We don't know why God preferred one over the other, but the point was that Cain had a choice going forward—to do what was right or to do what was wrong in the eyes of God.

Imagine that I ask two of my children to take out the garbage and the recycling. When they return, one has taken the garbage out, but the other has instead cleaned up the family room. While it is great that they have both done something helpful, one has done what I asked and the other has not.

Push this a little further: when the second child is still asked to take out the recycling, it helps no-one for him to storm off indignantly because he had 'helped' but just not in a way that was obedient. This may help us understand something about *love* and *obedience*.

Cain had a choice. He could do what was asked of him or not! If he did, it would be pleasing to God, yet even when he didn't do what was asked, he still had a choice. Instead of loving, he hated and took the life of his brother.

John uses this story to teach what true love really looks like. It is to love the other. For him, true love is love that is *both pleasing and acceptable* to God.

When John calls people to love each other, he calls them to love as children of God. Importantly, this love of others must be in a way that is pleasing and acceptable to God first. And to love in this way may not be a love that is accepted by the world. The world may therefore hate, like Cain (v 13).

What is it that the world wants you to love? The answer to that could be an almost endless list of possessions, ideals, lifestyles or behaviours. *How* is it that the world wants you to love? The answer to that will often be only in ways that are always approving and affirming. Whether or not those things or actions are good, the point John wants to make is that *Christian love is a sacrificial love for others that is both pleasing and acceptable to God before it is to the world*.

And here is a contrasting observation. The opposite to this kind of love may well be hatred, as demonstrated by Cain. But often the opposite to this Christian love is *fear*:

> There is no fear in love. But perfect love drives out fear, because fear has to do with punishment. The one who fears is not made perfect in love. (1 John 4:18)

If your love is Christian love, then there is nothing to fear. There is no punishment that goes with a love that is pleasing and acceptable to God. But if you taint that love—if you promote a love that is not pleasing and acceptable to God— then as it is a tainted love, it is logical that people will fear that kind of love.

It is not uncommon today (at least in Western societies) for Christians to be accused of being unloving. At times, what lies behind these accusations can be the fact that Christians have indeed *been* unloving. They have done something that was not pleasing and acceptable to God (e.g. physical, mental or sexual abuse, financial mismanagement, or anger—to name a few). If this is the case the accusation is well founded, and the Christian person should feel the weight of the rebuke or consequence.

At other times, however, what lies behind an accusation like this is not that the Christian has been unloving, but that they have been loving in a way that the accuser does not or cannot recognize as love. To offer a critique, if the world's view of 'love' is all about feeling personally approved of or affirmed, then people who belong to the world will struggle with the Bible's view of love. This view of love—the Bible's view—can be approving and affirming, yet also sees that it is still possible to love in rebuke or correction. In rejecting those things that are pleasing and acceptable to God, the accuser may have embraced things that the world has embraced, which are neither pleasing to God nor acceptable to him (e.g. materialism, some aspects of sexuality, individualism and terrorism—to name a few).

People will fear a love that they do not understand or accept.

Truth

So what does it look like for Christians to love others?

> This is how we know what love is: Jesus Christ laid down his life for us. And we ought to lay down our lives for our brothers and sisters. If anyone has material possessions and sees a brother or sister in need but has no pity on them, how can the love of God be in that person? Dear children, let us not love with words or speech but *with actions and in truth*.
>
> This is how we know that *we belong to the truth* and how we set our hearts at rest in his presence: If our hearts condemn us, we know that God is greater than our hearts, and he knows everything. (1 John 3:16-20)

Contrary to Cain's action, we see that Jesus laid down his life for others—for us. In fact, John uses this act as a way to define love. When Jesus stepped up to the cross, he did that as the only one who didn't need the cross to *make himself* acceptable to God. Why? Because in Jesus, we see the 'perfect Abel'.

Everything that Jesus did and said was pleasing to his Father; in him there was no sin (1 John 3:5; 1 Pet 2:22; Heb 4:15). When Jesus stepped up to the cross, he did it to *make others* acceptable to God. Jesus not only gave his life so that others might have life—he demonstrated what real love looks like.

Love doesn't destroy another's life. Love gives its own life that another might live. At the very least, you would have to say that this kind of love is self-sacrificial. It puts the needs of others before your own. For Jesus, it meant literally laying down his life. For many Christians across the ages, there have been numerous examples of people who have forfeited their lives for the sake of others.

For John, love is not a sentiment or an emotion. It is not merely words or platitudes. It is a love that costs, a love that is not looking for return, a love that may be undeserved, a love that is without self-interest, a love that gives, a love like that of Christ. Don't be like Cain. Be like Jesus.

And what directs this kind of love? Truth.

As Christians hold to the truth that they know in the gospel of Jesus, that gospel compels them to take action and live it out. That is what is means to "belong to the truth" (1 John 3:19). You cannot claim to belong to the truth if there is no evidence of your love for others. And you cannot claim to belong to the truth if you don't obey.

Christians demonstrate that kind of truth both inside and outside of the church family all the time—be it in the support offered for the needy, the care offered to those who are ill, the gifts given to those who are going without, or the response to appeals to help those across the world in want. It comes in the way folk listen to one another, encourage one another, and at times rebuke one another. It is demonstrated whenever someone serves—be that formally or informally, recognized or hidden.

Most people in society like the idea of being loving towards others. Christians want to demonstrate that love both truthfully and obediently.

And here, again, is a contrasting observation. If we let go of truth, then falsehood will diminish love because it will erode the very basis upon which love is built (see Eph 4:25).

If as a society we rip that which is true from its moorings and replace it with an 'alternative truth', then that will have an effect on the way we both understand love and live out our love. It will mean that as a society we will try to love in ways that are not pleasing or acceptable to God. And it will also mean that these ways of 'loving' will show themselves to be problematic, and in the end not really loving at all.

Christians must truly love, and we know how to do so because in Jesus we have true love demonstrated sacrificially. *Christian love is a sacrificial love for others that is both pleasing and acceptable to God before it is to the world.*

Obedience

What is this love that is pleasing first to God?

> Dear friends, if our hearts do not condemn us, we have confidence before God and receive from him anything we ask, because we keep his commands and do what pleases him. And this is his command: to believe in the name of his Son, Jesus Christ, and to love one another as he commanded us. The one who keeps God's commands lives in him, and he in them. (1 John 3:21-24)

A love that is pleasing to God is a love that obediently follows his commands. And with obedience comes the blessing of knowing that God is happy with us. It is not that we are earning his love; it is that we are living out what it means to be loved and love in return.

A parent recounted to me a comment that her son had made after he had done something wrong. He said to her, "I don't like you very much when I am doing the wrong thing!" Smart kid.

John says that if you are loving the way that God wants you to, then you should have every reason for confidence, knowing that he will be pleased. There is only a problem if you are not doing what pleases God. Love that is pleasing is when you are being obedient to his commands, particularly his commands first to believe in the name of his Son Jesus Christ and second to love one another.

I hope that sounds familiar, because it is what Jesus said when he was asked about the most important commandment: "'Love the Lord your God with all your heart, and all your soul and all your mind' ... and the second is like it: 'Love your neighbour as yourself'" (see Matt 22:37-39; Mark 12:30-31—we looked at these verses in the Bible study; cf. Luke 10:27).

If we ignore what is commanded of us, then what we are doing is putting our own desires before what God wants of us. That is simply showing us to be selfish, like Cain.

And here is another contrasting observation. If we let go of obedience, then selfishness will diminish love because it will put our own desires before those of both God and others.

Without obedience, it is impossible to demonstrate true love. *Christian love is a sacrificial love for others that is both pleasing and acceptable to God before it is to the world.*

• • •

In 1885, a Presbyterian minister in Edinburgh, the Reverend Robert Law, suggested three helpful tests from 1 John for anyone wanting to determine whether they are Christian. These can be seen as a **theological test**, a **social test** and a **moral test**.[13]

---

13 R Law, *The Tests of Life: A study of the First Epistle of St John,* 2nd edn, T & T Clark, 1909, Chapters XI (Righteousness), XII (Love) and XIII (Belief). It was from John Stott's discussion of Law's three "tests" that I took the categories of moral (Righteousness), social (Love) and theological (Belief); see JRW Stott, *The Letters of John,* IVP, 1988, p 58.

The **theological test** is to ask yourself: Do I *believe* that Jesus is the Son of God? If not, you are not a Christian (1 John 3:19, 23).

The **social test** is to ask yourself: Do I *love* others? If not, you are not a Christian, because God is love and it is clear that a loveless person does not know God (1 John 3:11, 4:7-8).

And the **moral test** is to ask yourself: Do I *practise* righteousness and the keeping of God's commands? If not, your claim to be a Christian should be challenged (1 John 3:22-24).

Each test is helpful. One focuses on *truth*, one on *love*, and one on *obedience*. And without all three, your claim to be a Christian could be questioned.

Genuine love

Love, truth and obedience are three Christian values that together help to define a Christian person. *Christian love* is love where truth is valued. *Christian truth* tells us how to obey. *Christian obedience* demonstrates true love.

Corrupt any one of those core ideas and you corrupt all of them. Replace love and you have *fear*. Replace truth and you have *falsehood*. Replace obedience and you have *selfishness*.

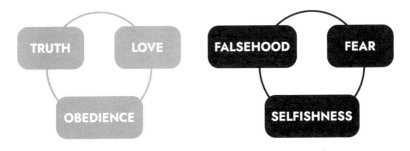

If you get *love* wrong, it will show itself in falsehood and self-ishness. If you get *truth* wrong, it will show itself in fear and selfishness. If you get *obedience* wrong, it will show itself in falsehood and fear.

So often, that is the picture that we see of society—fear, falsehood and selfishness.

The Christian alternative is to do the opposite. Love others, in truth, obediently. Essentially, the Christian is called to be genuine in relationships even if our love, truth or obedience is rejected, mocked or ignored by the world. "We love because [God] first loved us" (1 John 4:19).

Love in action

The apostle Paul (given that he was called out of a life of persecuting Christians into a life of serving God) understood the significance of what it meant to be loved sacrificially by Jesus. As a result, he was eager to live out that love and teach others to demonstrate real Christian love. In writing to the church in Corinth, he offered one of the most instructive and challenging descriptions we have of what Christian love in action should look like:

> Love is patient, love is kind. It does not envy, it does not boast, it is not proud. It does not dishonour others, it is not self-seeking, it is not easily angered, it keeps no record of wrongs. Love does not delight in evil but rejoices with the truth. It always protects, always trusts, always hopes, always perseveres. (1 Cor 13:4-7)

It is a compelling and attractive picture—a picture that even the harshest critic of the Christian faith may find hard to criticize. And so, with this picture of Christian love in mind, let us try and practically put love into action by way of some reflective questions to close this chapter:

- While your love for others will often be imperfect, how can you love others in ways like those described in 1 Corinthians 13?
- Are there personal preferences or philosophical objections that prevent you from seeing love as best expressed in ways that are pleasing and acceptable to God before the world?
- Are you protecting personal interests or comforts that you need to let go of so that you can fulfil your obligations to love God and love your neighbour? Can you put love into action even if it will cause you inconvenience?
- Are there opportunities that you have, or that you can create, to demonstrate sacrificial love for others regularly?
- How will you exercise Christian love towards someone who fears, rejects or falsifies the love that you offer?

In whatever practical ways you respond to this call to action, remember that it is the fact that God first loved us that should drive us to love one another (1 John 4:10-11, 19, 21). And remember that *Christian love is a sacrificial love for others that is both pleasing and acceptable to God before it is to the world.*

What's best next?
- What aspects of your thinking and your behaviour should be changed as a result of reflecting on this 'essential' Christian quality?

- What step can you take this week to make that change?

Pray about it.

8. GODLY IN GIVING

The world says: The more you get,
the happier you will be.

But God says: Give generously! Freely give,
for you have been given much.

A voice from Acts: "Where great grace is given, great grace should be shown!"

Inspired by Acts 4:32-5:11

On the surface, it all looked so good. But it turned out that God needed to teach us something about what's *beneath* the surface. And it wasn't easy.

We were all together, sharing and giving as we were able. There was such unity, such love—we were one in heart and mind, and there was no selfishness, no territorialism, no-one claiming that their possessions were theirs alone. Such generosity.

No-one went hungry. From time to time, one person or another would sell a house or a piece of land and bring the money to me or the other apostles. I lost count of the number of times I saw a bag of money placed at my feet and heard words like "Peter, please use this for anyone in need".

The joy we had in sharing what we had with everyone, and making sure all were cared for, was like nothing we'd experienced before—and it was so very different from how the world around us was used to working.

I don't know why this surprised me. As an apostle, I was testifying all the time about the death and resurrection of Jesus—and I knew, perhaps more than anyone, that where great grace is given, great grace should be shown! What was happening in the church was simply people knowing the gospel and living by it. Such an encouragement.

Encouragement. That makes me think of Barnabas. We gave him this name—meaning 'son of encouragement'—and it couldn't have suited him better. He was always looking for ways to care for others, including their financial needs. He was one of the people who sold property and gave away the proceeds, no strings attached. He sold a field and brought the money to us. He knew that the money really belonged to God, and should be used to do God's work. I can't help but be encouraged when someone does that.

Shortly after Barnabas made his gift, Ananias arrived and also dropped a bag at my feet. I looked inside. It was a large sum of money—the proceeds from the sale of some property. It looked so generous—just like what Barnabas had offered.

But that's when God stepped in to show us something more important than just how much money was there. The Holy Spirit saw inside Ananias; he knew that he and his wife, Sapphira, had kept back some of the proceeds from the sale.

That in itself was no problem. Whenever someone gave, it was up to them how much they offered.

But what Ananias and Sapphira did was try to deceive me, our church, and, worse still, God. They said they were giving all the money they'd received. They were using us to build their own reputations so that we would think they were being as generous as Barnabas. They weren't giving the money first and foremost to help others; they were giving it to make themselves look good before others. That is attempting to buy favour. That is the opposite of grace.

Of course, I didn't know all this when the bag was first laid at my feet. But almost immediately, prompted by the Holy Spirit, I found myself saying, "Ananias, how is it that Satan has so filled your heart that you have lied to the Holy Spirit and kept for yourself some of the money you received? You have not lied just to human beings but to God."

Ananias, shocked, opened his mouth to speak—but he didn't get a chance to answer God's rebuke, because right then and there he fell down dead!

We were stunned, of course. People standing nearby who had heard and seen what had happened were filled with fear. Some young men ran over to us, wrapped up Ananias' body and took him away to bury him.

We were still in shock and trying to come to terms with what had happened when, three hours later, Sapphira came in. She didn't know what had happened to her husband. Our hearts were breaking for her. But then again, God's Spirit made it clear to me that she, too, had come to us seeking to build her own reputation. I picked up the bag that Ananias had brought us, held it up, and said, "Tell me, is this the price you and Ananias got for the land?"

"Yes," she said, "that is the price."

She lied.

I shook my head, filled with sadness and anger. "How could you conspire to test the Spirit of the Lord? Listen! The feet of the men who buried your husband are at the door, and they will carry you out also."

And there, right at that moment, she fell down at my feet and died too!

In came the young men. They wrapped her and carried her out. And for a time, the church was seized by fear.

I can tell you, it took everyone a while to work through what had happened and accept God's will in this matter— but accept it we did. Sometimes there are hard lessons to be learned.

We all realized that being one in heart and mind cannot be just for show. If deceit, pride and betrayal lurk beneath the surface, no amount of money can make up for that. God sees our motives; and what he wants from us is real, meaningful, a sincere desire to put others' needs before our own—just like our Lord Jesus did. That's grace in giving. That's beyond generous!

Bible study

Reflection/discussion points

- How do you measure generosity?

- Is it normal for people to spend 'beyond their means'?

- What examples of selfless generosity have you seen in people?

Pray that this study would help you to hear the word of God and respond to it in a way that is pleasing to him.

Read 2 Corinthians 8:1-15

1. What attitudes have motivated the Macedonians to give?

2. Why do you think Paul calls giving an "act of grace" (vv 6-7)?

3. How is Jesus the supreme example of this grace? In what way was he rich? Is he giving material riches?

4. Verses 13-15 move from generosity to equality. How does this add to the discussion of giving?

5. What is the giving actually going to (v 14; see also 2 Cor 9:12)?

Read 2 Corinthians 9:1-15

6. Why is Paul sending the "brothers" in advance to the Corinthians and the church in Achaia (vv 3-5; cf. 8:6, 10-12)?

7. Is it right to say that Paul is more interested in *why* the Corinthians should be generous in giving than in *how much* they will give (vv 9:6-11)? What does he say God is interested in?

8. What else will result from their generosity (cf. 2 Cor 9:11b-15)?

Implications

- How does this challenge, change or shape your thinking about generosity to:

    (a) your local church?

    (b) the wider Christian community?

- What do you need to pray about concerning your generosity?

- Do you need to change your giving habits or patterns? If so, what steps do you need to take now?

Note: The Bible makes many mentions of wealth, greed and money. It is never in favour of money if it causes a person to give it higher value than they give to God. If you are interested in looking into this further, here are some references: 1 Chronicles 29; Prov 23:4-5, 30:7-9; Eccl 4:4, 5:10; Hag 2:6-9; Mal 3:6-9; Matt 6:1-4, 19-24 (cf. Luke 16:13); 19:16-30 (cf. Mark 10:17-31); Mark 12:41-44; Luke 6:20-26, 9:3-6, 12:13-21, 16:19-31, 18:9-14; Eph 4:28; Col 3:5-7; 2 Thess 3:6-13; 1 Tim 5:8, 5:18, 6:2b-19; Jas 1:10-11, 5:1-6; 1 Pet 5:1-9.

Suggestions for prayer

- Give thanks for the grace shown and given by Jesus.
- Pray for a right attitude towards material possessions and wealth, and ask for a generosity of heart to give.
- Pray that those who receive what you give would use those funds wisely and properly.

A blind spot?

Christians are givers. In fact, they are called to be godly in giving.

In this chapter, we will look at another area of life in which Christians are called to be different to the world around them. The world promises satisfaction and happiness in anything that money can buy, but God calls upon the Christian to give generously.

The battle, although played out before our eyes every day, is really a battle played out in our hearts and minds. Each day, all week, we get hit by an avalanche of advertising informing us of the best, newest, most economical, trendiest, most affordable, and most necessary products or services available—be they dining, travel, technology, fashion, real estate, entertainment, motoring or home furnishings. There is a lot competing for our dollar. Thank goodness we can earn to afford all these *necessary* things!

It is likely that people today digest more 'push' advertising (be it through social, visual or print media) than they do any other form of information. And if that is the case, then spare a thought for what that must do to our thinking as a society.

Don't get me wrong: advertisements do have a place—they tell us what is on the market, what it costs, and whether it is any good. I am not someone who is totally against a world of material things—in fact, especially on Father's Day, I am very thankful for some of the material things available to us!

Yet, as a society, we have a blind spot. It may not be just that we want to own things or experience more, but rather that our consumerism is driven by a desire to be *changed by our ownership* of the stuff. Let me explain.

The goal of marketing is to appeal to a person's desire. If the advertiser can convince you that your life will be better with the advertised product or service, then they have done their job. Successful marketing suggests to the consumer that if they have the product or service, then they *inherit* some of the product's or service's traits.

Look at *product advertising*. If you own that new phone, then you will be more efficient or slick, or be faster. If you are wearing that dress or those shoes, or carrying that handbag (as is that celebrity), then you will be more elegant or trendy, or appear to be younger. If you read that book, then you will be more intelligent or informed or up-to-date. If you drive that car, then you will be more professional or adventurous or advanced or stylish.

And look at *food and restaurant advertising*. Is it really about food? Most food ads sell the *idea* that we could become like the food or restaurant on offer—relaxed, dignified, alternative, simple, healthy, quick, sweet, slim or whatever particular quality the targeted consumer wants to be.

Or *travel advertising*: it's not just about the destination. It is about *becoming* calm, exotic, reflective, pampered, cultured, curious or experienced as a world traveller.

Or my favourite, *real estate advertising*. Buy this house or this property, in this particular area, near this particular school, with access to these neighbourhoods or shops or facilities, and you will be *seen* to be affluent, successful or able.

As a society we are driven to buy, because our ownership of things in some way changes us to be more like those things—or so we think! That is materialism: to value possessions or the collection of possessions as the means to fulfilment.

The purchase of those things in no way grants us a more secure hold on the desired state that we seek, but it might inspire in us a feeling that we are on the way to a better place, and so it helps us work harder to buy more of those things, because surely, one day, we might reach that imagined, enigmatic state.

The reason the topic of godly giving needs to be considered by the Christian person is because the Bible has a lot to say about giving and money, and what it says about giving is very different to what our world promotes.

Godly in giving

Christians are called to be godly in giving. That could be giving in attitude, time, energy or money—all are important. While other essential topics in this book address the way we give in attitude, time and energy, here we will focus specifically on the area of money and the way we generously and responsibly use the resources that God has put in our care.

Let me make four points from 1 Timothy 6 which may help our thinking.

1. Godly giving is *not* a means to financial gain

To teach that godliness in the area of giving will be a way to secure financial gain is to teach heresy. It is a false doctrine. It is not what our Lord Jesus taught.

Look at what the apostle Paul said to Timothy:

> If anyone teaches otherwise [i.e. false doctrines] and does not agree to the sound instruction of our Lord Jesus Christ and to godly teaching, they are conceited and understand nothing. They have an unhealthy interest in controversies and quarrels about words that result in envy, strife, malicious talk, evil suspicions and constant friction between people of corrupt mind, who have been robbed of the truth and who think that godliness is a means to financial gain. But godliness with contentment is great gain. (1 Tim 6:3-6)

This is a good double-check of my motivations in writing this, and also for any church when it comes to teaching about money. Giving should not be to make me or the church rich. Your giving should not be so that you might become richer.

When Paul wrote this, he wanted to make sure that the motivations that drove Timothy (who was charged with the responsibility to lead a church) were right ones. His point: when you teach those in your church, don't do it for financial gain.

Godliness when it comes to money looks different to the world around us.

So what does godliness look like?

2. Godly giving is connected with contentment

Contentment is a mark of godliness—see the last sentence in the passage from 1 Timothy above. I imagine that Paul takes his lead here from Jesus when he warns people about being more worried about riches in this world than about serving God. In Luke 12, Jesus helps a man to think rightly about riches and inheritance when he tells him the parable of the rich fool. This fool realized that he didn't have enough barn space to store his crops and grain (if he was around today, it might be his cars or tools or clothes or art collection!). So the man built more and more storehouses. But God said, "You fool! This very night your life will be demanded from you". After telling this parable, Jesus says, "This is how it will be with whoever stores up things for themselves but is not rich toward God" (Luke 12:20-21).

The point is that it is much more important to be rich towards God than rich in this world. How can you be content if you spend your whole life building a financial nest egg when you can't take the nest egg with you when you die?

The human life is not meant to be a life of making money or becoming rich. Why would it be? The greatest gift possible is the gift of life, and the greatest riches to enjoy are the riches that await us in the heavenly inheritance that comes when we die in faith or when Jesus returns for his faithful ones.

That means that, for now, we should be living within our means and focusing on looking after God's affairs while he looks after ours. Jesus shows the man to whom he's talking in Luke 12 that a person's life "does not consist in an abundance of possessions" (v 15). The author of Hebrews writes: "Keep your lives free from the love of money and be content with what you have" (Heb 13:5).

Now, while in God's eyes *affluence* is unimportant, Jesus is not saying *possessions* are unimportant. There are basics that are necessary, which are mentioned in 1 Timothy 6— food and clothing:

For we brought nothing into the world, and we can take nothing out of it. But if we have food and clothing, we will be content with that. Those who want to get rich fall into temptation and a trap and into many foolish and harmful desires that plunge people into ruin and destruction. For the love of money is a root of all kinds of evil. Some people, eager for money, have wandered from the faith and pierced themselves with many griefs.

But you, man of God, flee from all this, and pursue righteousness, godliness, faith, love, endurance and gentleness. (1 Tim 6:7-11)

The issue arises when we place the *luxuries* before the *necessities* and so get lost in the add-ons. Paul warns that a very real temptation and trap is to want to get rich. Money will inherently tempt, and the risk is that it will lead a person to place their hope in things that have no eternal meaning.

In our secular world, the way decisions are made is very often based first and foremost on the protection of our wealth—we give little, we chase after a bargain, we seek higher wages. In the country I live in, our policies about border protection, our tax system, the pursuit of owning property, the desire to be in an economic surplus (COVID put that ideal to bed!), and the drive to maximize profit margins are all examples of putting wealth and wealth protection before people. Why? Ironically, so that we can maintain a lifestyle, or protect ourselves in case things get really bad, or enjoy ourselves more and more.

It is a dangerous deception!

"The love of money is a root of all kinds of evil." Paul is not saying that *having money* is a root of all kinds of evil (though it may be the expression of all kinds of evil). He is saying that a root of all kinds of evil is *loving money*. And the risk, which the Christian needs to be very aware of, is that some people who love money or are eager for money have wandered from the faith and pierced themselves with many griefs. Can you see the paradox here? The desire to get more wealth to protect ourselves is the very thing that will pierce us with many griefs. That is like buying a weapon to protect yourself only to find that the weapon inadvertently becomes the very thing that harms you!

So Paul says to the Christian: you person of God, flee from the love of money and pursue things that have other-person-centred value—righteousness, godliness, faith, love, endurance and gentleness. All things that are hard to put a price tag on.

Contentment is more important that affluence.

3. Godly giving means putting your hope in God

There is another problem with affluence: it is unreliable. Paul's advice to Timothy is this: "Command those who are rich in this present world not to be arrogant nor to put their hope in wealth, which is so uncertain, but to put their hope in God" (1 Tim 6:17). Riches can come quickly and can be lost just as fast. We all know stories about losses incurred due to stock market crashes or natural disasters or theft or misadventure. And even if we avoid those financial dangers, we will still lose those riches: either we will get so old that they are no longer of any use to us, or we will die.

Money tempts us. It asks us to put our trust in it, yet it is such an uncertain thing in which to put our trust! So a better way is to put our hope in God who gives richly and provides everything for our enjoyment.

Proverbs 23:4-5 puts it a little more eloquently:

Do not wear yourself out to get rich;
    do not trust your own cleverness.
Cast but a glance at riches, and they are gone,
    for they will surely sprout wings
    and fly off to the sky like an eagle.

Sounds simple, but it is a fundamental test of faith for someone to recognize that the hours and effort, the salary or wage, the work goals or KPIs, are not as important as living trusting that God has *your life* under control.

4. Godly giving means being rich in good deeds, generous and willing to share

If you want to be rich, then be rich! Be rich in good deeds:

> Command them to do good, to be rich in good deeds, and to be generous and willing to share. In this way they will lay up treasure for themselves as a firm foundation for the coming age, so that they may take hold of the life that is truly life. (1 Tim 6:18-19)

Paul closes off his letter telling Timothy to command his church to do good, to be rich in good deeds, and to be *generous and willing to share.*
What does it mean to be generous and willing to share?

Generosity is a wonderful demonstration of love. Being generous comes with a cost. You pay so that someone else benefits. In fact, the best example of generosity comes in the gospel. God gives his Son, at great personal cost, so that we might freely live.

Christians are called to be generous in that same manner.
To be generous means to give even though there may be

a personal cost, so that others receive freely. God gives not so that we can be affluent, but so that our needs are met; in fact, so that our *greatest* need is met—we are saved from our sin.

Therefore, when Christians give, it is not so that others will be affluent, but so that others' needs are met, and so that their greatest need (that they are saved from sin) is met.

A few years ago, a husband and wife asked to see me to talk about their giving. There was some financial pressure in the household and some disagreement about the best way to use and give the money that they had. The husband had a hard and fast rule: "We give 10% because the Bible says so". The wife wanted to know whether that figure could be revised because she was struggling to provide the necessary basics for the family with the amount that she had to spend. So I talked to the husband about the 10% tithe being an Old Testament principle.[14]

It is an imperative that the person of God is generous with what they have been given, both in giving to the work of the gospel and in providing for those in need. I wanted to affirm him in what he gave, yet help him to recognize that he still had a responsibility to his family.

I then asked him what he did with the other 90% of his salary. At that point, his wife jumped in and said: "75% is

14 In the Old Testament, a 'tithe' was asked of Israel to give the first ten per cent of whatever they produced or earned (grain, fruit, wine, olive oil, herd, flock, honey) to the Lord in thanks for and recognition of his provision and their dependence upon him (Lev 27:30-33; Deut 14:22-26; 2 Chr 31:2-8). Some of the offerings would be used to support their Levitical priests in their work serving at the tent of meeting and later in the temple (Num 18:21; Deut 14:27). Note that the priests were also expected to tithe (see Num 18:25-29). Every three years a further tithe was asked of Israel in order to care for the foreigners, the fatherless and the widows living among them (Deut 14:28-29).

used on the mortgage. He wants to pay that off as fast as possible!" Now, I'm not a financial adviser. I am sure there is wisdom in paying your home loan off really quickly; but let me suggest that you should make sure both your family and your giving are higher priorities than getting out of a home loan! In fact, Paul gave Timothy similar advice (see 1 Timothy 5, especially verse 8).

The one who is rich became poor, so that those who are poor might become rich—not materially but eternally (see 2 Cor 8:9). Christians do not give to make others affluent; they give because they are commanded to be rich in good deeds, generous and willing to share—just like the Lord Jesus.

Organizing your giving

Over the generations, across the world, all the way to your local church family, there will be numerous examples of godly and generous givers. Among those who have given are many who have given even at times of extreme poverty or hardship (Luke 21:1-4; 2 Cor 8:2). It is right and proper to be immensely thankful to God for these saints (maybe you are one such person). Under God, what has been given has served the gospel and those the gospel has reached for centuries. Godly giving, although rarely put on display, is a wonderful testimony to the power and gift of the gospel. Praise God!

So how should a Christian organize their godly giving?

Let's look first at our *priorities* and then at the *practical mechanics*.

Godly giving priorities

The way people give often comes down to a question about priority. When it comes to financial giving it is not uncommon for Christians to organize their giving with the wrong order of priorities. At a basic level, it goes something like this:

1. Start with *income*.
2. Deduct *expenses*.
3. Deduct *savings*.
4. Then work out what is left over to *give*.

While it may still be a generous amount that is given, the point is that thinking about expenses and/or savings before giving is an order of priorities that betrays a lack of willingness to share. That may sound harsh. But think about the priority that is being fed: *income* is what I earn, *expenses* are what I spend (on me), *savings* are what I retain (for me) and *giving* is what I give (to others). This way of thinking hardly puts others before oneself.

Perhaps a sounder (and, dare I say, more Christian) way of ordering our priorities would look like this:

1. Start with *income*.
2. Prayerfully work out what you think you should *give*.
3. Deduct *expenses*.
4. Then put what is left towards your *savings*.

If it does not add up, then it could be that expenses or savings are too high. I say that because generosity means very little unless it challenges the luxury of our own lives and comforts. It may mean that you need to cut back on expenses, or reduce the amount that you save, and then if it still does not add up, your giving will need to be reviewed. Generosity is not measured in the amount you give as much as it is measured by the sacrifices you make in giving.

Godly giving mechanics

Now let's talk about the actual mechanics. What follows here is an attempt to show how the thinking behind godly giving takes place practically—six steps to put theory into practice.

Step 1: Pray

Working out what to give, who to give it to, and when and how to give are all good concerns and require a degree of godly wisdom. Alongside this should be a desire to be content in any and every situation (see Phil 4:11-13). Contentment is something that needs to be prayed for (and learned) as we set our hearts on the treasures of heaven. This whole exercise should be given to God in prayer. How? Here are some examples:

- Ask God to show you where to give and for opportunities to give.
- Ask God to help you prioritize giving before expenses and saving.
- Ask God to use what you give for gospel purposes.
- Ask God to continue to provide for you.

You get the idea.

Step 2: Work out your income

Tax time is a good time to do this. Add up your total income amount. Include in this figure whatever incoming funds you receive (e.g. wage, salary, stipend, government benefits, income from property or investments, bonuses, the notional value of any fringe benefits).

Step 3: Work out what word-based ministries you want to support financially

I say *word-based* because there are so many good organizations asking for money.[15] If you cannot meaningfully support all, then one way to choose between them is to support those who are intentionally and unapologetically seeking to proclaim Christ through the preaching of his word.

They may be organizations of which you are a member, your church being the most obvious example. And they could be organizations with which you have some kind of history or an interest in supporting—a university or tertiary ministry, a mission organization, a theological college, a ministry training organization, a child sponsorship charity, a Bible translation organization, an outreach ministry (i.e. to city workers, bush or school ministry, homeless mission) … and the list could go on.

Step 4: Work out how much to give

Now look at the numbers and work out what support you want to give to each of your chosen ministries, starting with your church. Fairly quickly, you'll work out that a '10% tithe' is not going to stretch that far. Rather than working out how much you give based on a 10% guideline, just work out how much you want to give! The percentage is less important.

---

15 Good secular organizations will attract financial support from both non-Christian and Christian donors; however, it is very unlikely that most good Christian organizations—especially those primarily focused on proclaiming God's word—will attract significant financial support from non-Christians.

Step 5: Work out your costs—your expenses and desired savings
This is often where our attitudes to personal comforts will be challenged. You know the amount that you want to give away (step 4), so when your list of expenses gets added in, plus the amount that you are aiming to save, it will become quite clear whether the numbers add up. By looking at the costs you can work out what, if anything, needs to be cut back. There are all sorts of expenses that can get the chop if needed.

This is a good step to work through slowly and creatively. Give some thought to what you spend, challenging yourself to determine what is *necessary*, what is a *preference*, and what is a *luxury*. Cutting back (reducing your spending), limiting (reducing the frequency of something) and ceasing (stopping something) may all be options. You may also be able to work out ways to make costs lower (e.g. using vouchers, making rather than buying meals, cashing in reward points).

Now, this step may very well show that your *necessary* costs cannot be covered. If that is the case, then you will need to return to step 4 and reduce the amount that you intend to give.

Step 6: Adjust your electronic giving
In the country where I live, the ability to set up electronic giving is a gift. You have worked out both the organizations to which you want to generously give and the amounts, so setting up the electronic schedule means that you can set and enjoy—at least until the next tax time. Of course, knowing that you have a schedule set to ensure regular giving should not prevent you from giving at will to whatever

additional gospel causes may come across your path each year.

• • •

There you go. Not rocket science, but hopefully reflective of gospel priorities, and a system that helps you to be godly in giving. How you organize your giving is up to you, but bear in mind: Christians are givers. We are called to be godly in giving. So be wise and intentional and generous for the sake of the gospel which saved you.

What's best next?

- What aspects of your thinking and your behaviour should be changed as a result of reflecting on this 'essential' Christian quality?

- What step can you take this week to make that change?

Pray about it.

9. FRUITFUL IN SERVICE

The world says: Take what you can get
and look after yourself.

But God says: In love, find ways to do good works
for others (even if it costs you).

A voice from Acts: "I was called to serve."

Inspired by Acts 20:13-38

It was the last time we saw him.

When Paul sent for us, we were eager to see him again. He'd journeyed to Ephesus and spent time with us twice before, and we had learned so much from his words, and from the way he served us. So of course, when he sent for us, we—the whole eldership of the Ephesian church—were happy to travel to Miletus to see him again.

From the moment we arrived, there was a sense of heavy significance about this occasion—it was like a 'last will and testament' moment. Paul knew that trouble was ahead of him. And it was very clear that he wanted to leave us with some final instructions so that we might know how to continue in the faith and service of our Lord Jesus.

I will never forget what he told us. Like a father speaking kindly but seriously to his children, he talked to us about service.

"You know how I lived the whole time I was with you", he said. "I served the Lord with great humility and with tears."

This was true. He had. We had seen him stand firm even though he had been challenged by Jewish opponents plotting against him. What pain he must have suffered to be treated in this way by his own people! Yet he had not hesitated to preach anything that would be helpful to us, and he had taught anyone who would listen—Jews or Greeks. And so many had turned to God in repentance and faith.

And then Paul told us what he thought might happen next—both to him and to us.

He was very conscious that his days were numbered. "I am going to Jerusalem, not knowing what will happen to me there. I only know that in every city the Holy Spirit warns me that prison and hardships are facing me."

We'd all heard about the many troubles that Paul faced wherever he went to serve. But he kept going in spite of it all, and he told us why: "I consider my life worth nothing to me if only I may finish the race and complete the task the Lord Jesus has given me—the task of testifying to the good news of God's grace".

Paul was a picture of humble service. We had seen that over and over again. Not only had he been the first to proclaim the gospel to unbelievers; he had also served us, the leaders of the church. And he reminded us of this, saying, "I have not hesitated to proclaim to you the whole will of

God". He had thoroughly prepared us so that we also would be ready and able to serve—just like him.

And to us he now said, "Watch over yourselves and all the flock of which the Holy Spirit has made you overseers".

He was reminding us that we were shepherds. Wise words. As a leader now in the church of God, I was called to serve and care for my flock, and it was Paul who had shown me how to do that in a Christlike way.

But I suppose it's easy to forget, sometimes, that some of the work of a shepherd is hard, and even frightening—even though Paul had warned us about this before. And it was a warning that Paul turned to next, his tone becoming even more serious.

"After I leave, savage wolves will come in among you and will not spare the flock."

He went on to tell us that even people from our own church family would arise and distort the truth in order to draw away disciples after them. He told us to be on our guard.

Was that always going to be part of the deal? Would we have to cope with people trying to undo Paul's work, our work—trying to lure people away from the truth that we had been called to proclaim?

We were deeply troubled by these sobering words. And we knew right then that serving our Lord was going to require much of us; and that for all the good that would be done, there would also be much pain for those who would serve.

We would need to be selfless. It would require humility.

A silence fell as we digested all that he had said.

But Paul, sensing our distress, gave us all the assurance we needed. He committed us to God, and to the word of his grace, knowing that it was God's word above all else that had built us up over the years and would continue to do so.

And Paul reminded us, too, that he had shown us the way to serve. We knew what to do, because of how he had been with us. He had not let silver or gold or clothing distract him from serving. He had worked to supply his own needs so as not to be a burden. He had modelled the kind of hard work that we would have to do to serve the weak. He had lived by the words that our Lord Jesus had lived by: "It is more blessed to give than to receive".

He'd said earlier in the day that he'd never see us again. But I don't think it really sank in until the moment he stood and said that he had to go. We all wept as we embraced him and walked with him to the ship waiting in the harbour, grief-stricken that we would never see his face again. It was very hard knowing that, in all likelihood, he was going to his death as he continued in service of the gospel.

What he left with us, though, can never be taken from us. In Paul we saw the kind of service that our Lord Jesus himself showed us. Jesus humbled himself to the point of death, so that those he died for might be exalted. Paul humbled himself to death, so that those he served might be exalted in Jesus. And he asked us to humble ourselves, even in the face of hardship, so that those we serve might be exalted in Jesus.

I hope that we, and those who come after us, will always follow the example of Jesus in humble, fruitful service.

Bible study

Reflection/discussion points

- If you could sum it up in one sentence, what would you say is the whole purpose of the Christian life?

- What is the difference between 'faithfulness' and 'fruitfulness'?

Pray that this study would help you to hear the word of God and respond to it in a way that is pleasing to him.

Read Matthew 5:13-16

This passage occurs at the beginning of the "Sermon on the Mount" where Jesus is specifically teaching his disciples while the gathered crowds listen in (cf. Matt 5:1, 7:28). As part of his teaching, he uses two metaphors: "You are the salt of the earth" (v 13) and "You are the light of the world" (v 14).

1. What is the point of the "salt of the earth" metaphor? (If it helps, Jesus uses the idea of "saltiness" in relation

to discipleship on two other occasions: Mark 9:50 and Luke 14:34.)

2. What is the point of the "light of the world" metaphor?

3. How are the disciples called to apply these two metaphors?

4. What is a "good deed" (v 16) and what makes it Christian (given that anyone in the world can do good deeds)? If unsure, have a look at Matthew 22:37-40.

Read John 15:1-17

5. Jesus uses another metaphor here to describe the Christian life: that of the vine and the branches. Who is the vine? Who are the branches?

6. Several times in this passage Jesus calls for the disciples to "remain in [him]". What do you think he is asking?

7. What is the fruit that Jesus is looking for here? What kind of fruit will be lasting?

8. Is it possible to be faithful but fruitless?

Implication

How do passages like these challenge your understanding of Christian service?

Suggestion: Be creative—come up with a list of fun and creative ways to do good works that will shine a light before those who are stuck in the dark. Pick one and do it.

Suggestions for prayer

- Give thanks that you have a gospel that both calls you and gives you good reason to serve in the name of Jesus.
- Pray that you would have the willingness to serve others.
- Pray that you would be intentional in creating opportunities to do good works for the benefit of those who don't yet know Jesus. And pray that those works will be seen to be distinctive because of him.
- Pray that your efforts would bear Christlike fruit that lasts.

The gift of God

Service is the Christian 'family business'. To be *fruitful* in service is the aim.

We have almost come full circle. That fundamental truth, that a Christian is *saved by grace and not by the good works that they do*, means that we arrive at this last essential topic with a small tension. Saved by grace, full stop. Yet called to do good works.

Before looking at this last topic, allow me to address this tension for a moment. As we previously considered, being a person of faith in Jesus is not a status that is earned or established by doing some wonderful deed, by enduring suffering, by forgoing things, by attending church, or by giving funds. Being a person of faith is a gift from God and the result of the work that Jesus has first done.

The apostle Paul says to the church in Ephesus:

For it is by grace you have been saved, through faith—and this is not from yourselves, it is the gift of God—not by works, so that no-one can boast. For we are God's handiwork, created in Christ Jesus to do good works, which God prepared in advance for us to do. (Eph 2:8-10)

In just a few verses, Paul puts "good works" in their rightful place. Salvation is a gift. Like any gift, it comes from a giver. Those who, in faith, accept the gift do not receive the right to boast about it or take credit for it.

Think about the nature of a gift. It is given, sometimes at great cost to the giver. Yet it costs the recipient nothing (otherwise it's not a gift!); it is given freely for their benefit. Paul recognizes this reality in the gospel. Salvation is a gift, given at great cost by God the Father when he offered up Jesus, his only Son, freely for the benefit of all whom he died for.

Now the question: How will that great gift be received?

I was once given a very flashy pen, beautifully inscribed with my name. It was a good gift. It was costly gift—but there was no cost to me. The person who paid the price was the person who generously gave me the pen.

There are several ways that I could have responded. One option was to give it back: "No thanks, I don't want it". My loss. A second option was that I could have taken it and then forgotten about it: put it in my drawer for another day. Nice pen, but while it collected dust in my drawer it would make no difference to my life. A third option was that I could have misused it. Although it was a nice pen, it could have doubled as a makeshift dart for my dartboard. I am not sure how the person who gave it would have felt about me using such an expensive pen in a way that was never intended.

Or, of course, I could have accepted the gift, thanked the person who gave it to me, and then used it as intended—as a pen!

Allow me to use this story to explain the relationship between grace and good works.

God gives many gifts, his best gift being salvation in Jesus Christ.

Some fail to see the value of the gift at all. They *reject* it. Their loss.

Others take it, but effectively *forget* about it, and it makes no difference to their lives.

Still others grab the gift, but *misuse* it. This is the kind of person that Paul speaks against: someone who wants the free gift of salvation but who uses it to claim some kind of credit. Perhaps they consider that their "good works" make them deserving of the gift. Or perhaps they boast about what they do as if their works somehow keep them saved.

The final response—and the appropriate response—is to *accept* the gift and to use it as intended.

This appropriate response to a good gift is Paul's point in Ephesians 2:10: "For we are God's handiwork, created in Christ Jesus to do good works, which God prepared in advance for us to do". The way to receive the great gift of salvation is to accept it, be thankful, and then live in the light of that gift as God intended—that is, do the good works that God prepared for the person of faith to do. The Christian is called to do good works and to serve—not in order to *gain* salvation, but *because of* their salvation.

Now, of course, anyone can do a "good work". You don't have to be Christian to do works that are good, which is why there are numerous examples around the world of people doing wonderful deeds for the sake of others. So what is distinctive about *Christian* good works? The answer: Christian good works serve both God and others and bear lasting fruit for the Lord.

This chapter is all about how the Christian disciple should use the good gifts that God has given to be *fruitful in service*.

Work in creation

To help us understand how and why good works are so important, let's go right back to the beginning of the Bible, when God created humanity. In his perfect creation, there was much to enjoy. And it was all good, including the work:

Then God said, "Let us make mankind in our image, in our likeness, so that they may rule over the fish in the sea and the birds in the sky, over the livestock and all the wild animals, and over all the creatures that move along the ground."

So God created mankind in his own image,
in the image of God he created them;
male and female he created them.

God blessed them and said to them, "Be fruitful and increase in number; fill the earth and subdue it. Rule over the fish in the sea and the birds in the sky and over every living creature that moves on the ground."

Then God said, "I give you every seed-bearing plant on the face of the whole earth and every tree that has fruit with seed in it. They will be yours for food. And to all the beasts of the earth and all the birds in the sky and all the creatures that move along the ground—everything that has the breath of life in it—I give every green plant for food." And it was so.

God saw all that he had made, and it was very good. And there was evening, and there was morning—the sixth day.

Thus the heavens and the earth were completed in all their vast array.

By the seventh day God had finished the work he had been doing; so on the seventh day he rested from all his work. Then God blessed the seventh day and made it holy, because on it he rested from all the work of creating that he had done. (Gen 1:26-2:3)

There is a lot going on in this important passage. At the pinnacle of his creation, God creates humanity in his image and blesses them. What we see is an open relationship where God and man dwell together. He gives them everything, including a job: they are to rule over all living things—the fish, the birds, the livestock and wild animals, all earthbound creatures, every plant and tree.

We get the sense that what God gave was meant to be for the benefit of both humanity and the creation all around. In ruling over the world, humanity was called to act under God, to rule in a way that both honoured God and reflected his image for the benefit of everything under his authority as Creator. And when God looked at all that he had made, *his work*, he proclaimed it "very good". God is a worker.

Further on in Genesis 2, the Garden of Eden is described as a home with all kinds of trees "that were pleasing to the eye and good for food" (v 9). But not only is God a worker; he also creates people to be workers. In placing the man in this perfect garden, he gives him a job—"work [the garden] and take care of it" (v 15)—along with a command—"You are free to eat from any tree in the garden; but you must not eat from the tree of the knowledge of good and evil, for when you eat from it you will certainly die" (vv 16-17).

Imagine a great palace—the kind of place that would be fit for royalty. Ballrooms with floor-to-ceiling windows; dining rooms with the best silverware; a library with every title you could imagine; kitchens with fridges and pantries stuffed full of every kind of delicacy; bedrooms with four-poster beds, each with a decadent ensuite. Grounds with perfectly manicured lawns; tennis courts; the most enormous pool; stables; rose gardens with every variety and colour possible; and more. The lap of luxury.

Now imagine that, in the middle of the garden, stands a locked shed with a sign: "No entry, for your own safety".

Genesis 1 and 2 paint a picture of an even better dwelling than this palace and its grounds; a world where God lives with humanity as they enjoy all that God has given them— all, that is, except that one tree. It is as if God has said, "Join me and enjoy; it is my gift to you. I ask only that you care for the world I have given you, and as you do, don't touch the tree that I know will hurt you."

In creation, we see what God expects of humanity. This gift comes with the expectation that it is used in accordance with God's intention. And while God invites humanity to enjoy all that he has offered, his expectation is still that people will work and be obedient to what God commands. To be able to work (as God did) is one of his gifts. And so is rest. Just as God rested from his work of creating in Genesis 2, in the fullness of time he would also invite humanity to enjoy the blessing of rest from their work, and to use this time of rest to remember God and his blessings (see Exod 20:8-11).

Of course, it does not take long for humanity to mess it up. In the very next chapter (Genesis 3), blessing turns to curse. Adam and Eve, tempted by the devil in the form of a serpent, eat from the only tree that they were told not to eat from. As they eat, they do indeed gain knowledge of good and evil, for they discover just how bad evil can be. It hurts.

It is as if they have ignored the palace and all the grounds and decided to focus their attention on the shed. They disregard the warning and break in, only to discover everything that they don't like or want.

As a result, God bans them from the perfect garden (Gen 3:22-23). Their work, once fruitful, becomes laboured. This is the first example of someone taking a gift and using it badly. What had been perfect is now damaged. The open relationship between God and humanity is now closed. The same result will be experienced by all who follow.

After living like royalty, humanity finds itself thrown out of the palace and escorted from the grounds—no longer able to enjoy the luxuries of living and working at the best address ever.

But there is good news. The tragedy of Genesis 3 is not the end of the story. God does not wash his hands of humanity. Instead, he puts into place a rescue plan—a plan that goes from Adam right through to Jesus. By word and promise, God gives his people a way back into a perfect relationship with himself. God may have rested from his work of creation, but now he begins his work of salvation.

Work in salvation

God's work in salvation would ultimately bring humanity back to the palace, where they would be restored into a position in which they could enjoy working and living with all the blessings of royalty. For they would be brought home with the king.

The unfolding story of the Bible takes us on this journey. God has created his world; humans have fallen into sin; and from that time on, the story of the Old Testament shows us the people of God (Israel) going through ups and downs that fundamentally repeat what has happened in Genesis 1-3.

Just as he blessed Adam and Eve in the garden, God blessed his people—be it with a *promise* (like those which he gave to Noah, Abraham, Moses, David and Jeremiah), a *provision* (like children, freedom, protection, food, water, victory, land and more), or a *command* (like the Ten Commandments, or speaking his word through his chosen agents like the judges, kings and prophets). But even as God offered one blessing after another, the people of God took those promises, provisions and commands and either *ignored* them, *forgot* them or *misused* them—just like Adam did.

They failed. They failed to do the work that was asked of them or to serve in the way that was required. The result: the people of Israel found themselves repeatedly at odds with God, living under a curse rather than enjoying his blessings. It is a pattern that repeats over and over and over.

Until Jesus.

Jesus came to rule in a way that modelled the image of God. In fact, he was to be called "Immanuel", which means "God with us" (Matt 1:23). Immediately following Jesus' baptism, he was led into the wilderness, where he was tempted for forty days and nights:

> Then Jesus was led by the Spirit into the wilderness to be tempted by the devil. After fasting forty days and forty nights, he was hungry. The tempter came to him and said, "If

you are the Son of God, tell these stones to become bread."

Jesus answered, "It is written: 'Man shall not live on bread alone, but on every word that comes from the mouth of God.'"

Then the devil took him to the holy city and had him stand on the highest point of the temple. "If you are the Son of God," he said, "throw yourself down. For it is written:

> "'He will command his angels concerning you,
>> and they will lift you up in their hands,
>> so that you will not strike your foot against a stone.'"

Jesus answered him, "It is also written: 'Do not put the Lord your God to the test.'"

Again, the devil took him to a very high mountain and showed him all the kingdoms of the world and their splendour. "All this I will give you," he said, "if you will bow down and worship me."

Jesus said to him, "Away from me, Satan! For it is written: 'Worship the Lord your God, and serve him only.'" (Matt 4:1-10)

The comparison with Adam is striking. While Adam is in a garden of provision, Jesus is in the wilderness of want. Both are tempted by the devil, yet Adam and Eve trip at the first hurdle. Jesus, on other hand, while hungry, is offered bread but refuses, for to use his power for his own desires would be to rule in a way that *rejects* his Father. Jesus is then placed at the high point of the temple and told to jump as a way to 'prove' his importance to God. Again he refuses, for to put God to the test would be to *misuse* the access he had to his Father. Jesus is then taken to a high mountain lookout and shown all the kingdoms of the world in all their splendour. They will all be his, if only he will deny God; it's an invitation to *forget* him. Jesus is once again unmoved by this final lie.

Unlike Adam and Eve, Jesus holds to what God said.

Three times he is tempted; three times he says, "It is written" to show that he lives under God's word. His final reply shows what it truly means to 'rule' under God: "Worship the Lord your God, and serve him only" (Matt 4:10; cf. Luke 4:8).

At this point, Jesus' public ministry began. His message was "Repent, for the kingdom of heaven has come near" (Matt 4:17; cf. Mark 1:15). The work of bringing people back home had begun. Jesus was calling people back to the palace, back to the garden, and into a relationship where they could dwell with God forever.

In Jesus, we have the visible model of how to live as one who worships and serves the Lord. As the instructor for his disciples, and by extension for all those who would follow, Jesus showed how to serve both God and others, and how to bear fruit for the Lord.

Fruitful works

It did not take long for the people to take notice of Jesus. He saw the gathering crowd, perched himself on a mountainside, and delivered what has become known as the "Sermon on the Mount" (Matthew 5-7). He began to teach what is essential in discipleship.

In the sermon, Jesus uses fruit as a metaphor to instruct his disciples in how they should live. He says that the external fruit that comes from what a person does will tell you whether they are internally good or bad:

> "Watch out for false prophets. They come to you in sheep's clothing, but inwardly they are ferocious wolves. By their fruit you will recognize them. Do people pick grapes from

thornbushes, or figs from thistles? Likewise, every good tree bears good fruit, but a bad tree bears bad fruit. A good tree cannot bear bad fruit, and a bad tree cannot bear good fruit. Every tree that does not bear good fruit is cut down and thrown into the fire. Thus, by their fruit you will recognize them. (Matt 7:15-20; cf. Luke 6:43-45)

If "false prophets" are motivated by what is bad and wrong, then the outcome of their actions will eventually show their error (for it is impossible for good fruit to come from a bad tree). Conversely, if a disciple is motivated by what is good and right, then the outcome of their actions will eventually show their quality (for good fruit can only come from a good tree). The same measure applies to both: "by their fruit you will recognize them".

You will notice that this fruit is obvious to all. Everyone can see the difference between a grapevine or fig tree that produces fruit that can be enjoyed and a thornbush or thistle that offers nothing of value.

In John's Gospel, that fruit analogy is picked up again when Jesus calls himself the true vine and his disciples the branches (as you saw in the Bible study).[16] In saying this, he wants his disciples to "bear much fruit", showing themselves to be his disciples and, in doing so, giving the Father glory (John 15:5-8). In fact, he has appointed them so that

---

16 There is a wider contrast in view here. In Scripture, the people of God (Israel) were previously described as a "vine"—yet in the Old Testament this vine is always described as fruitless, useless and marked for destruction (see, for example, Ps 80:8-19; Isa 5:1-7; Jer 2:21; Ezek 15:1-8). The reason: Israel were continually unfaithful. When Jesus calls himself the "true vine" in John 15, he picks up on the Old Testament promise that the people of God would be restored (Isa 27:2-6). Jesus is the true and faithful vine and, as a result, fruitful as intended. And so when he calls his disciples to "remain in" him (a repeated phrase in John 15), he is saying that they must also bear good fruit.

they will "go and bear fruit—fruit that will last" (John 15:16).

What is the fruit? It is that they will love others; specifically, that they will love others in such a way that everyone will know that they are disciples of Jesus (John 15:17; cf. 13:34-35). Yet how is it that fruit lasts? An act of love today may be forgotten tomorrow in the same way that the fresh fruit that I buy today (if it remains in my fruit bowl long enough) will eventually perish.

The lasting fruit referred to in John 15 is the loving efforts that draw others to Jesus so that they also might enjoy the life that comes with being part of the true vine. And as they then take their places as disciples of Jesus, they too are called to "bear fruit—fruit that will last".

While it took a while for the disciples to catch on, they clearly did, for there are numerous places in the New Testament (written by the disciples of Christ) where instructions are given to individuals or to the church at large to do good deeds that will bear fruit.

In Colossians, it is Paul's prayer that believers will "live a life worthy of the Lord and please him in every way: bearing fruit in every good work" (Col 1:10).

The Galatians are told that "the fruit of the Spirit is love, joy, peace, forbearance, kindness, goodness, faithfulness, gentleness and self-control" (Gal 5:22-23).

Paul tells the Corinthians to "give yourselves fully to the work of the Lord" (1 Cor 15:58) and to "abound in every good work" (2 Cor 9:8).

Timothy is instructed to teach believers to "do good, to be rich in good deeds" (1 Tim 6:18).

Titus is to tell those who have been redeemed and purified in Jesus Christ to be "eager to do what is good" (Titus

2:14) and then he is to call them to "devote themselves to doing what is good" (Titus 3:8).

The Christian family in Hebrews is called to "spur one another on toward love and good deeds" (Heb 10:24).

And James, the brother of Jesus, suggests that "faith by itself, if it is not accompanied by action, is dead" (Jas 2:17).

All this is to say that Christians are called to do good works—that is, works that will last. They know the gift that comes with salvation in Jesus. To accept this wonderful gift is to then use what you have been given in a way that serves God and serves others. And the aim should be to bear fruit for the Lord by calling people to Jesus in word and deed.

Works of service

So what do good works that are acceptable to God look like?

Again, Jesus is the best model.

When James and John, two of Jesus' disciples, requested the positions of honour at his right and left hand, Jesus offered them a lesson in humility:

> "Whoever wants to become great among you must be your servant, and whoever wants to be first must be slave of all. For even the Son of Man did not come to be served, but to serve, and to give his life as a ransom for many." (Mark 10:43-45; cf. Mark 9:35; Matt 20:26-28)

Jesus uses 'servant' and 'slave' language to describe the attitude he expects of his disciples. It is hard to get up in arms about this request when he himself took that very path—he came not to be served but to serve. For Jesus, greatness is seen in the way his disciples serve.

As we draw near to our conclusion, let's get practical and think about good works that can serve God in three different ways:

- giving glory to God
- bringing those who are not yet disciples to God
- helping those who are disciples give glory to God.

Of course, many of the essential topics that we've already covered have included acts of service. So allow me to offer three key categories, along with some diagnostic questions, that may help as you consider some of the many ways in which you could do works of service.

1. Serve the Lord in a way that gives glory to him

First, in whatever way you serve, it should be in such a way that it gives glory to God.

"Let your light shine before others, that they may see your good deeds and glorify your Father in heaven" (Matt 5:16). The implication of what Jesus says here is both horizontal and vertical. The Christian does good deeds before others whom they are serving (horizontal); but the driving purpose behind the good deeds should be that they cause the recipient to offer praise, not to the doer of the good deeds, but to God, the originator of good deeds (vertical). Do good works for others to the glory of God. Conversely, while recognizing that the Christian is not perfect, watching your behaviour before others is helpful because when you fail, your deeds may cause people to question God—and this is hardly glorifying.

Colossians 3:23-24 says:

> Whatever you do, work at it with all your heart, as working for the Lord, not for human masters, since you know that you will receive an inheritance from the Lord as a reward. It is the Lord Christ you are serving.

In our human context, your work is primarily for the Lord Jesus. Whatever you do, whether in word or deed (Col 3:17) or in what you eat and drink (1 Cor 10:31), should be done in the name of the Lord Jesus and for the glory of God. And there is a wonderful freedom that comes with this reality. Whether or not your work is appreciated by others, the way you serve will still be recognized by the Lord.

There are many codes of football played around the world, some of which have barely any resemblance to others. In my part of Sydney, the local National Rugby League (NRL) team is called the Penrith Panthers. Each week during football season, thousands gather to watch grown adults spend 80 minutes running at one another until they collide—hard. Whatever your preferred type of football, one thing that all codes seem to have in common is eager supporter bases. People who follow their favourite team will arrange their week so that they can go to the game or watch it on TV, dress up in their team colours, and post team news and images on social media to show their support. The language they use is all about ownership and commitment: "This is *my* team"; "*We* are the Penrith Panthers". They give glory to their team because their actions and words are saying "I follow this team"—in fact, "I am part of this team".

The Christian is called to be a committed, passionate supporter of Jesus. There are many ways that this support and allegiance can be indicated, but the best way is to ensure that your words and deeds point people to the one you follow. Serve in such a way that it is obvious that you are on 'Team Jesus'. The result: glory goes to God.

And so, as you make decisions about how to use your gifts, time and energy, some good questions to ask are: *Will this work of service bring glory to God? How can I do this work of service in a way that draws attention not to me but to my Lord and Saviour?*

2. Serve the Lord in such a way that others may give glory to him

Work out ways to serve those who are not yet disciples so that they may see the value and benefit of being a disciple themselves.

Writing to displaced and scattered Christians, the apostle Peter said: "Live such good lives among the pagans that, though they may accuse you of doing wrong, they may see your good deeds and glorify God on the day he visits us" (1 Pet 2:12). Despite being persecuted for their faith, these Christians are called to serve even those who may be the persecutors. The quality of their life is on display such that even the person who wants nothing to do with faith in God is caused to praise its value.

History is full of examples of believers fulfilling this command as their Christian convictions drove them to serve and help others. The establishment of hospitals, schools and charities (to pick just three examples) has often been the result of Christians wanting to serve the community in a way that reflects Christ. While it is true that some of these establishments have eventually become secular in their approach, and some have done such a poor job that their deeds are now quite clearly seen as bad deeds, the point still stands. Live such good lives that outsiders will give the credit and glory to God.

That will only happen if the disciple serves in ways that address a felt need, and does so in a way that clearly demonstrates their faith motivation. Consider your workplace, your school, college or university, your sports club, your neighbourhood, voluntary services or charities, the military reserves, and so on.

As you make decisions about how to use your gifts, time and energy, it is good to ask these questions: *Can I serve the world around me in a way that will open doors for people to consider faith in Christ? How can I make a difference in the lives of those who don't know Jesus?*

3. Serve the Lord in such a way that helps other disciples give glory to him

Finally, serve in ways that will help other believers to live for Jesus.

The apostle Peter is again helpful. In speaking to the church family, he says:

> Each of you should use whatever gift you have received to serve others, as faithful stewards of God's grace in its various forms. If anyone speaks, they should do so as one who speaks the very words of God. If anyone serves, they should do so with the strength God provides, so that in all things God may be praised through Jesus Christ. To him be the glory and the power for ever and ever. Amen. (1 Pet 4:10-11)

This is a call to use the various gifts and skills that God has given us to care for those in the family of God. Will that always be easy, or convenient, or exciting? Experience will tell you that will not always be the case. Serving others takes time and energy, yet that is what is asked of those who have received God's grace (his gifts) in its various forms. And notice that God gives the strength to enable you to carry out these works of service.

Disciples of Jesus should put service before convenience, serving in a way that speaks the very words of God, so that in all things, he might be praised through Jesus.

The church (both local and universal, as we saw in chapter 6, 'Committed in membership') is a good place to serve. Most churches have many and various ways in which members can serve, and many use rosters to organize the ways people serve. Rosters may be an efficient way to organize the formal ways people serve, but if the sum total of the mission or ministry activity that happens in a church is limited to only the times that people serve on rosters, that is a poor gathering of believers indeed.

I am often inspired by the way Christians serve around church, yet I also recognize that the motivation behind acts of service can vary greatly. For some, serving only happens when it is convenient (and, as such, may not happen at all if something better arises). For others, serving happens under obligation (and, as such, is determined by when their names appear on a roster). But for others, serving happens because they are passionate about using their gifts and skills to build up the family of Christ (and, as such, they own the cause and are committed to the task). While the specific task of service will vary greatly (both up-front and behind the scenes), it is the cause of Christ that should motivate us as we serve in many and various ways together.

All Christians are called to serve. Use whatever gifts you have received to serve others, and do it in such a way that it helps them also give glory to God.

And so, as you make decisions about how to use your gifts, time and energy, some good questions to ask are: *What can I do to serve with my church family? How can I serve in a way that draws minimal attention to myself and maximum attention to the Lord Jesus?*

If you don't know how or what you could do, ask someone in leadership. One of Christ's gifts to the church is the gift of those who give shape to mission and ministry—the apostles, prophets, evangelists, pastors and teachers (Eph 4:11-12). Their job as ministers of the word is not to do all the works of service, but "to equip [Christ's] people for works of service, so that the body of Christ may be built up" (Eph 4:12).

Conclusion: in service of the king

One final comment as we close. We serve today because tomorrow is coming.

At the last supper, as Jesus was preparing to make that ultimate sacrifice and head to the cross, he taught his disciples to serve with the future in mind:

> The greatest among you should be like the youngest, and the one who rules like the one who serves. For who is greater, the one who is at the table or the one who serves? Is it not the one who is at the table? But I am among you as one who serves. You are those who have stood by me in my trials. And I confer on you a kingdom, just as my Father conferred one on me, so that you may eat and drink at my table in my kingdom and sit on thrones, judging the twelve tribes of Israel. (Luke 22:26-30)

Note the 'kingdom' language here. As with all kingdoms, the king (or monarch) is the most important person. Yet in this kingdom, the one who rules is the one who serves. To draw out the implication, Jesus describes a royal table at which those who have served with him are to enjoy the eating and drinking expected at a royal banquet. He is painting a picture of what is in store for all those who are with him (even through the trials). Here is a king who serves, and who gives to his disciples the banquet of all banquets.

To return to the previous illustration of the great palace with beautiful grounds, it is because of Jesus, the king, that his people have been brought back, not only to the grounds or into the great palace, but to the royal banquet table, at home with the king.

The Bible closes by describing a new home for the people of God (see Rev 21:1-5 and following). The garden is transformed into a city; a new heaven and new earth, one where the dwelling place of God is now among his people. It's a picture of provision even beyond that in the Garden of Eden; a picture of security without the risk that it could all be taken away as we saw in Genesis 3. And on the throne, as promised, is the one who is making "everything new". The servant king. Jesus.

Now, like this king, the disciple is called to serve. For *service* is the Christian family business, because that is what Jesus asked of his disciples—then and now, and until he returns.

What's best next?

- What aspects of your thinking and your behaviour should be changed as a result of reflecting on this 'essential' Christian quality?

- What step can you take this week to make that change?

Pray about it.

AFTERWORD

When I walk into my father-in-law's shed, I find a wonderful collection of tools—in fact, so many that I have no idea what they are all for. But I have a job to do. So I grab a toolbox and throw in a hammer, a screwdriver, a tape measure, some pliers, a drill, gloves, a torch, and a pencil. I am ready to go. I have the specific tools I need to get the job done. While there are many and varied tools in that shed, these are the specific and essential tools that I know I need to use to effectively complete the job.

Throughout this book, we have looked at nine essential aspects that any person of faith in Jesus needs to grasp to do the job that Christ asks of his disciples. We started with what it means to be *saved by grace*, this essential truth operating like the 'toolbox' that holds all the subsequent aspects that are essential in discipleship. In looking at what it means to be *grounded in the Word, faithful in prayer, bold in witness, resilient in suffering, committed in membership, loving in relationships, godly in giving* and *fruitful in service*, we have considered many of the 'tools' that are essential for any disciple as they live out their Christian faith.

The aim here has not simply been to become a more

efficient Christian so that you can streamline what you do and minimize the effort required to live out your faith. Rather, the aim has been to consider what we must do so that, together with others in the family of believers, we might help one another live as *effective* disciples of Christ. And what Christ asks of his disciples is that they live in such a way that others notice their impressive way of life— so much so that they give the glory to God:

> Let your light shine before others, that they may see your good deeds and praise your Father in heaven. (Matt 5:16)

So pick up the toolbox, and take it with you—for as practical as all of these *essential* elements have been, they will mean nothing if you do not *do* something with these tools. Under God, go and do what you must: be a shining light before others. And to God be the glory.

APPENDIX A: IS THE BIBLE RELIABLE?

How can I trust that what was written down in the Bible is reliable?

If you could not be present at an event, what factors would you find helpful to establish the truth of that event today?

Eyewitness and witness records

It would help if someone who was there wrote down a recollection of the event—of what they saw and heard. In fact, it would be even more helpful if several people wrote down their recollections of that event.

At a simple level, that is what we have with the Gospels—the eyewitness accounts about Jesus at the beginning of the New Testament. Some who were there wrote down what they saw and heard—like Matthew (who wrote the Gospel of Matthew) and John (who wrote the Gospel of John). On top of those, we also have others who got to write down what they heard from those who were there—like Mark (who wrote the Gospel of Mark and who was the likely scribe for

Peter, who was there), and Luke (who wrote the Gospel of Luke after interviewing many who saw and heard Jesus). In the Gospels, we have the eyewitness and attested witness accounts of Jesus.

Copies of eyewitness and witness records

What else would help? Further to those written eyewitness records, it would help if those accounts were carefully copied, many times. The fact that many people take those important written recollections and copy them multiple times adds to the historical reliability of the original event. The presence of many copies tells you something of the importance of the original event. And the presence of copies in different languages tells you something of the significance and influence of the original event.

When you have many copies, you also have the ability to check for errors in transmission. Whenever something is copied, errors can be made, but with many copies, you can compare them and see clearly whether errors have been introduced or not (e.g. if four copies say one thing and a fifth contains a difference, it is likely that the fifth is in error).

When it comes to Scripture, be it the Old or New Testament, there are multiple copies of the original documents to compare. Speaking just of the New Testament accounts, literary scholar Bruce Metzger, in an interview with investigative journalist Lee Strobel, said this:

> We have what are called uncial manuscripts, which are written in all-capital Greek letters ... Today we have 306 of these, several dating back as early as the third century ... A new style of writing, more cursive in nature, emerged in roughly

AD 800. It's called minuscule, and we have 2,856 of these manuscripts. Then there are also lectionaries, which contain New Testament Scripture in the sequence it was to be read in the early churches at appropriate times during the year. A total of 2,403 of these have been catalogued. That puts the grand total of Greek manuscripts at 5,664.[17]

Strobel then recounts an additional piece of information that Metzger offered:

> In addition to the Greek documents, he said, there are thousands of other ancient New Testament manuscripts in other languages. There are 8,000 to 10,000 Latin Vulgate manuscripts, plus a total of 8,000 in Ethiopic, Slavic, and Armenian. In all, there are about 24,000 manuscripts in existence.[18]

The introduction to one edition of the Greek New Testament helpfully provides the total list of manuscripts, along with what part of the New Testament they record (be it a Gospel, Acts of the Apostles, a general epistle, a Pauline epistle or Revelation), their storage location in the world, and their attested date. The papyrus, uncials, minuscules, lectionaries and various language versions are all listed.[19]

Testing the eyewitness and witness records

What other factors would help you establish the truth of an event? It would help if the written accounts could be tested.

The passage of time should not make the witnessed

---

17 L Strobel, *The Case for Christ*, Zondervan, 1998, p 81. Copyright © 1998 by Lee Strobel. Used by permission of Zondervan (www.zondervan.com).
18 Strobel, *The Case for Christ*, p 81.
19 B Aland (ed) et al., *The Greek New Testament*, 4th edn, Deutsche Bibelgesellschaft, 1998, pp 1-29.

recollection of an event any less reliable, although it is not uncommon for someone to assert that because something is old it becomes superseded (my grandmother would have a problem with that!).

On the contrary, the passage of time can often help shore up the reliability of those written down witness recollections. We live in an age when we can reliably examine and carbon date the copies that we have. For example, we can look at each manuscript and compare the handwriting consistencies, the quality of the ink used, the age of the paper or scroll—and if they match up, they should all point to the same time period, which in turn shows the document to be authentic (or not).

With the attested date of the manuscript, it is then possible to consider the time gaps between the original event or document and the copy that survives. Testing the documents is helpful.

The earliest Gospel manuscript in existence is dated around AD 125, which means this copy was made only 92 years after the original event (from the date of Jesus' death in AD 33). There are other papyri which are dated around AD 200 (4 manuscripts), in the 2nd century (one manuscript), in the 3rd century (30 manuscripts), in the 4th century (22 manuscripts), in the 5th century (8 manuscripts), in the 6th century (14 manuscripts), in the 7th century (13 manuscripts) and in the 8th century (2 manuscripts). That means that there are 95 New Testament manuscripts dated less than 800 years after the actual events.

Compare that to the next most reliable ancient document in history—Homer's *Iliad*, composed about 800 BC, of which there are only 643 copies. The oldest surviving fragments of *The Iliad* are dated in the second and third centuries (approximately)—a gap of 900 to 1000 years.[20]

External sources

Are there any other factors that may help establish the truth of an event? Yes. How about other sources (friendly or not) that can attest to the truth of the original event? This could be other articles that make mention of it, or material evidence, or circumstantial connections that help establish dates or personnel involved.

For example, looking at coins, artworks, architecture, histories, novels, newspaper clippings, court reports and the like can often testify to people or concerns of an earlier time, even if the main features, purposes or topics of those items might be something or someone else.

In the case of the New Testament there is a wealth of helpful external source material—no novels or newspaper clippings, but plenty of surviving material from the time prior to, during and following the life of Jesus. It is helpful that there is much evidence mentioning people present or events occurring around the time of Jesus. For example, there are coins bearing the face of Caesar Augustus (called Octavian) who was in power at the time of Jesus' birth (see Luke 2:1) and Caesar Tiberius who lived at the time of Jesus' death (see Luke 3:1). There are historical writings such as those from Josephus (a Jewish historian) who wrote much about the

---

20 Note: I have been helped here by John Dickson's discussion, 'Is the New Testament Trustworthy?' in J Dickson, *Simply Christianity: Leader's Manual*, Matthias Media, 1998, pp 33-34.

people, issues, politics and geography of the time of Jesus.

It is even more helpful that there are external sources who mention Jesus himself—not because they believed in or followed him, but because he was a historical figure of the time that they wrote about. Josephus, in his *The Antiquities of the Jews*, names Jesus and mentions that his brother was James, that Jesus was called Christ, that he was wise and virtuous, that he had disciples, that he was condemned to death by crucifixion at the hands of Pilate, and that he appeared to have risen three days later.[21]

And there are also references that attest to the effect that Jesus had on people of the time. For example, Pliny the Younger (a lawyer and Roman governor of Bithynia) in his letters wrote about how, under the threat of death, he cross-examined the disciples of Jesus and asked them whether they thought Jesus was indeed 'a god'. Their affirmation would lead to their execution![22]

Suetonius (a Roman historian) wrote the histories of twelve successive Roman rulers and, when writing about Emperor Claudius, mentioned that Jewish Christians in Rome caused disturbances at the instigation of 'Chrestus' (another way to write 'Christ').[23]

Tacitus (a senator under Emperor Vespasian and governor of Asia) wrote about the fire that destroyed Rome in AD 64 and how the then Emperor Nero blamed it on the Christians—those who followed 'Christus', a man who had

21 Flavius Josephus, 'Jewish Antiquities', 18.3.3 and 20.9.1 (dated AD 93) in W Whiston (trans), *The New Complete Works of Josephus*, Kregel Publications, 1999.
22 Plinius Secundus (Pliny the Younger), *Epistulae* X.96 (dated around AD 112).
23 Gaius Suetonius Tranquillas, *The Twelve Caesars (De Vita Caesarum): Life of Claudius* (dated around AD 120).

been put to death during the reign of Tiberius at the hands of the procurator Pontius Pilate.[24]

These external sources all help to attest to the reliability of the New Testament accounts about Jesus—his life, his ministry and his impact.

Those factors that would be helpful in establishing the truth of an event today are all factors we can look to when trying to establish the truth of the Bible records. We are on firm historical ground when we pay attention to the Bible.

24 Cornelius Tacitus, *Annals* (dated around AD 116).

APPENDIX B:
IS EVERY CHRISTIAN
CALLED TO BE AN
EVANGELIST?

As we saw in chapter 2, 'Grounded in the Word', the apostle Paul wrote to his friend in 2 Timothy and instructed him to "preach the word" (4:2). He went on to say:

> But you [Timothy], keep your head in all situations, endure hardship, do the work of an evangelist, discharge all the duties of your ministry. (2 Tim 4:5)

In chapter 4, 'Bold in witness', we considered Colossians 4:2-6, written by both Paul and Timothy:

> Devote yourselves to prayer, being watchful and thankful. And pray for us, too, that God may open a door for our message, so that we may proclaim the mystery of Christ, for which I am in chains. Pray that I may proclaim it clearly, as I should. Be wise in the way you act toward outsiders; make the most of every opportunity. Let your conversation be always full of grace, seasoned with salt, so that you may know how to answer everyone.

Both of these passages present a call to do *evangelism*; that is, to proclaim the gospel of Jesus Christ.

From time to time there is a little bit of discussion among

Christian folk about how broadly this call to evangelism goes. Is every Christian called to be an 'evangelist'?

It is possible to read these verses and declare that evangelism is the duty of *all* who believe the gospel and that *every* believer should be taking *every* opportunity to share the news about Jesus with *everyone* they can. That seems to be Paul's expectation of Timothy.

It is also possible to read these verses and suggest that the duty of all who believe the gospel is to live a godly life, leaving the evangelism to those who are *gifted evangelists*. Paul and Timothy are clear that they want prayer for that very endeavour, but they seem to leave out the imperative for the church in Colossae to do the same.

Both arguments are logical and have merit. What could be said at a minimum is that all believers should *care* about evangelism and should *pray* for evangelists proclaiming Christ. Further, since these verses emphasize the interactions with those who are "outsiders" (those who don't yet have faith in Christ), it is clear that every believer is called to engage wisely with those who don't believe, making the most of the various opportunities they have to do so.

The opportunity to evangelize is as relational as it is circumstantial. Speaking the gospel will at times be to those you know well and at other times to those you have only just met—and then everyone in between. And speaking the gospel may sometimes happen in formal public settings and at other times in informal private settings.

For those who know you better (those with whom you have the most relational currency), you have more 'tools' at your disposal when it comes to evangelism: your words, your actions, your history, and the passage of time. They know you well, so there should be many things about your life that speak of Jesus. Your 'evangelism' will happen over longer periods of time as you take up opportunities to invite them, speak to them, live for them, and show them in love that it is a wonderful thing to know and trust Jesus. The relational circumstance means that you have far more opportunity to speak the gospel into their lives than those who might be 'gifted evangelists'. Expecting someone else to evangelize those you know and love most is hardly making the most of every relational opportunity.

Paul may be acknowledging that some people (like Timothy and himself) have many opportunities for *formal evangelism*—that is, the appointed public proclamation of the gospel that may be the 'job' of an evangelist or a minister or a speaker. That fact, however, does not relieve all Christians from the obligation to make the most of the many opportunities for *informal evangelism*—that is, the responsive, relational gospel conversations that arise through the normal circumstances of life.

Not every Christian is called to be a missionary *by occupation*; but every believer is called to be on God's mission *by pre-occupation*.

ACKNOWLEDGEMENTS

This book has been born out of recurring pastoral concerns. I am a pastor. I love opening the Bible and seeing people do business with Jesus and then grow as his disciples. What you have read in this book has been written first and foremost for those who want to do business with Jesus—either to check him out, or to understand how to live as his disciples, or to address doubts or concerns, or simply to make sure they are doing what they must as his disciples. My prayer is that what has been presented here will prompt you to look at Jesus and then look at your own life and consider what is essential in faith.

Books don't write themselves, and rarely are they a solo activity. There are many people who have given shape to this book and it is only right that they be acknowledged.

I am so thankful for the members and leaders of both Trinity Church Adelaide and Lower Mountains Anglican Parish, Sydney. It has been and is my privilege to serve in ministry alongside these many saints. It is these two groups who have heard me think and teach through the essential topics explored here. I am indebted to both churches for their grace and engagement as they have helped to shape the content of what you have read. Of particular note are Dave Swan, Rachael Connor, Luke Brush, Joshua Ord, Helen Brown, Trevor Oakley, Howard Whitehouse, David and Kathi Cohen, Jared Lidgerwood, Trace Akankunda, Arthur Ang, Michelle Schultz, Peter Evans, Cheryl Chapman, Shane Ellery, Katy Annis, Jill Phillips and Caroline Litchfield.

Along the way, various versions of this material have been reviewed, either upon request or in the course of ministry. I am thankful for those who have given their time, edits or suggestions, including Stephanie Lockery, Oliver Tweeddale, Naomi Beames, Cameron Phillips, Naomi Noakes, Mark Glew, Roger Yerramsetti, Josh Apieczonek, Anthony Elyard, Marnie Trebilcock, Mark Smith, Rachel Norman, Nick Lindeback, Josephine To, Paul Johnson, Lachlan Swan, Will Ramsay, Rebecca Snelson, John Maddock, Dan Carter, Jared Bartlett, Rebekah Ord, Lyn Krimmer, Bec Legge, and many others who have gone through the material while being discipled by someone.

The sharp eyes of Lisa Neale and Geoff Robson, who have edited this work and taken my words and massaged them into a far more helpful form, are deeply appreciated. And without the encouragement and persistence of the team at Matthias Media you would not be reading this, and so I am thankful for Ian Carmichael, Emma Thornett and Patrick Johns, among others, who have prompted and prodded along the way.

Behind many of the principles covered in this book sit those who have discipled me in faith—brothers whom I am eternally grateful for, including Mark Charleston, Rick Smith and Paul Harrington. Under God, they have shaped me as a Christian and as a minister, and I am sure that much of what they have taught me has been indirectly worked into the content of what I've written and is now unwittingly claimed and presented as my own ideas! Thank you, brothers.

This book is dedicated to my grandmother Glad Prothero, my mother Jan Noakes, and my wife Naomi Noakes— women who continue to point me to Jesus and call upon me to live my life for him. And to Naomi, along with Jeremy, Edison, Annika and Talitha—I love you.

Feedback on this resource

We really appreciate getting feedback about our resources—not just suggestions for how to improve them, but also positive feedback and ways they can be used. We especially love to hear that the resources may have helped someone in their Christian growth.

You can send feedback to us via the 'Feedback' menu in our online store, or write to us at info@matthiasmedia.com.au.

❀matthiasmedia

Matthias Media is an evangelical publishing ministry that seeks to persuade all Christians of the truth of God's purposes in Jesus Christ as revealed in the Bible, and equip them with high-quality resources, so that by the work of the Holy Spirit they will:

- abandon their lives to the honour and service of Christ in daily holiness and decision-making
- pray constantly in Christ's name for the fruitfulness and growth of his gospel
- speak the Bible's life-changing word whenever and however they can—in the home, in the world and in the fellowship of his people.

Our resources range includes Bible studies, books, training courses, tracts and children's material. To find out more, and to access samples and free downloads, visit our website:

www.matthiasmedia.com

How to buy our resources

1. Direct from us over the internet:
   – in the US: www.matthiasmedia.com
   – in Australia: www.matthiasmedia.com.au

2. Direct from us by phone: please visit our website for current phone contact information.

3. Through a range of outlets in various parts of the world. Visit **www.matthiasmedia.com/contact** for details about recommended retailers in your part of the world.

4. Trade enquiries can be addressed to:
   – in the US and Canada: sales@matthiasmedia.com
   – in Australia and the rest of the world: sales@matthiasmedia.com.au

Register at our website for our **free** regular email update to receive information about the latest new resources, **exclusive special offers**, and free articles to help you grow in your Christian life and ministry.

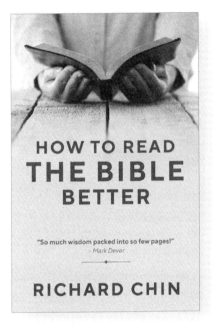